GREENWICH VILLAGE

A Guide to America's Legendary Left Bank

Acknowledgments

The author gratefully acknowledges the contributions of Tom Gitterman, Katherine Kaplan, Lynda Liu, Eliza Scott, David Stonehill, Mia Ting, and Adele Ursone. Special thanks to Barbara Cohen, my partner at New York Bound, and to Alexandra Stonehill, for perfectly capturing Greenwich Village in her photographs.

Greenwich Village: A Guide to America's Legendary Left Bank is part of a series of New York Bound books.

First published in the United States of America in 2002 by
UNIVERSE PUBLISHING
A Division of Rizzoli International Publications, Inc.
300 Park Avenue South
New York, NY 10010

02 03 04 / 10 9 8 7 6 5 4 3 2 1
ISBN 0-7893-0702-2

Editor: Ellen Rosefsky Cohen
Designers: Paul Kepple and Timothy Crawford @ Headcase Design

Printed in Singapore

GREENWICH VILLAGE

A Guide to America's Legendary Left Bank

By Judith Stonehill

For John

CONTENTS

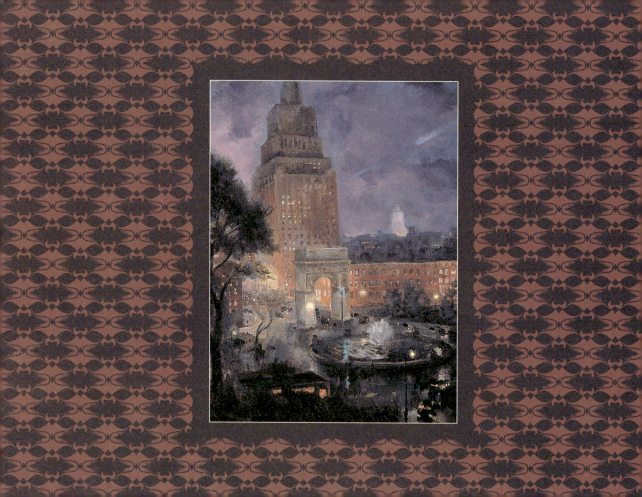

GREENWICH VILLAGE:
The Exhilarating Proximity

Greenwich Village of persistent legend—partly real, partly fantasy—is known for bold accomplishments and cultural greatness, daring ideas and fierce individuality. This is a place where things began: bohemianism, the little theater movement, abstract expressionism, beat poetry.

America's only Left Bank was created by an exhilarating proximity of playwrights, novelists, poets, painters, sculptors, and musicians. Whether accomplished or unknown, acclaimed or still promising, they congregated in studios, literary salons, tearooms, bars, and coffeehouses for camaraderie and a frenzy of talk. For each, there was always what one Village writer called "the memories of great lives and the possibilities therefore."

Greenwich Village, after all, is where Eugene O'Neill staged his earliest plays, Willa Cather wrote six novels, and Walt Whitman caroused with his newspaper cronies. Winslow Homer had a studio here, as did Thomas Eakins, William Merritt Chase, John Sloan, Isamu Noguchi, Edward Hopper, Willem de Kooning, Jackson Pollock, and countless other painters and sculptors.

The boundaries of the Village run north to 14th Street, west to the Hudson River, south to Houston Street, and east to a border that has roved over the decades from Broadway to a point still farther east. The idea of the place has always been so powerful, though, that geographical boundaries sometimes seem irrelevant.

The four walking tours in this book take you through Greenwich Village to the streets where the artists and writers lived and worked, as well as the places that they wrote about or painted during the century between the 1850s and the 1950s.

(Opposite) John Sloan. *Wet Night, Washington Square.* 1928. Delaware Art Museum

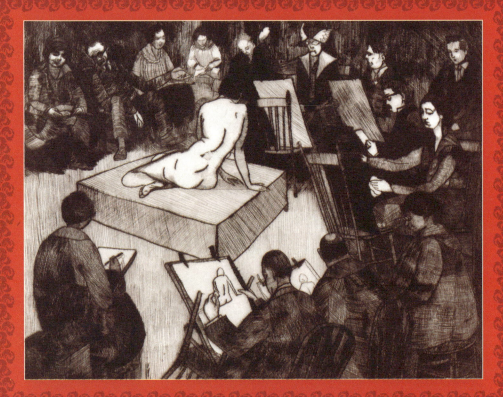

A CULTURAL CHRONICLE

Taking a walk through Greenwich Village is also taking a walk through time. The sedate brick houses that turn a dark rose color at the end of day evoke an earlier era when horse-drawn cabs and trolleys criss-crossed the city, when women carried parasols and children played with hoops. This picturesque Village, with its cobblestoned streets and small unexpected gardens, casts a spell, just as it always has on the artists and writers living here.

Turn any corner and the past is there—particularly the myths of the past that are as enduring as any of the nineteenth century buildings. From the earliest years, as Herman Melville looked inward for inspiration in writing his novels, to a century later, when Edward Hopper depicted an overwhelming sense of solitude in his painting, a legend was created about the individual and often lonely pursuit of creativity taking place in the Village.

The larger legend, though, always centered on the convergence of talent and ideas, the tumultuous outburst of artistic and literary creativity that occurred during certain decades in Greenwich Village. These fabled times took place in the late 1850s, and again in the early decades of the twentieth century, and still again from the late 1940s into the '50s.

Imagine, then, walking about the streets of Greenwich Village in 1859: the Tenth Street Studio had opened the year before at 51 West 10th Street, with twenty-five artists' studios and a large exhibition hall. On Saturday afternoons, visitors could stop by to view Albert Bierstadt's landscapes or Richard Morris Hunt's latest architectural plans or simply wander from one studio to the next to see the work in progress. Over 12,000 viewers stopped by to see Frederic Church's immense panorama *Heart of the Andes*, which he'd sold for $10,000—the most ever paid for an American painting.

(Above) Detail: *Artists' Reception at the Tenth Street Studios*, published in *Frank Leslie's Illustrated Newspaper*, January 23, 1869. The Museum of the City of New York
(Opposite) Peggy Bacon. *The Sketch Class*. Etching. 1919. Kraushaar Galleries, New York

There was new interest in art and literature during the prosperous years preceding the Civil War. By then many of the wealthy merchants had built handsome new red-brick houses on Washington Square, as the city tenaciously expanded north to 14th Street.

Anyone who wanted to buy art or look at paintings came to this area. There were auction houses on Broadway and the National Academy of Design on Fourth Avenue. On Thursday afternoons, art lovers could visit the city's first important collection of paintings, housed in galleries above a stable on West 8th Street. This concentration of artists, art collectors, patrons, dealers,

Early Bohemian Gathering

art schools, and their faculty created a burgeoning art colony in Greenwich Village.

The Cooper Union for the Advancement of Science and Art had just opened on Astor Place, in 1859. New York University was well established by then, having built its gabled and turreted white marble Gothic building on Washington Square eighteen years earlier. Space in this building was rented out to local artists and faculty members (although the art professor Samuel F. B. Morse complained about "the wetness of the walls when it rained").

In the late 1850s, a lively group of writers opposed to New England's literary conservatism began to congregate at Pfaff's beer cellar on Broadway, just a few streets east of Washington Square. The editors and writers of the *Saturday Press*, the controversial literary publication that printed Walt Whitman's poetry and Mark Twain's early stories, promoted Pfaff's as the headquarters of the bohemians. When Emerson was introduced there by Whitman, he found its denizens to be "noisy and rowdy firemen."

To be bohemian was a phrase dramatized by Henry Murger in *Scènes de la Vie de Bohème,* much read at that time, describing artists and writers of a certain type—talented and able, but as yet unknown. Many of the painters, sculptors, poets, and writers working in Greenwich Village in 1859 would fit this definition. By the turn of the century, though, bohemianism had come to mean a way of life that rebelled against tradition, reveling in bold ideas and unconventional behavior.

ॐ ॐ ॐ ॐ ॐ

In the early 1900s, the Village became known as "an American Bohemia or Gypsy-minded Latin Quarter." A new wave of rebels had arrived, drawn by the Village's reputation as a lively, creative place. "We came," one of them said, "because friends of ours had come already and written us letters full of enchantment."

The Village was soon thronged with free-spirited young people eager to embrace all the new causes: radical politics, individual freedom, sexual experimentation, and avant-garde literature and art. This exuberant time produced astonishing activity: the first group exhibition of "The Eight," whose bold realism jolted the public and critics alike in 1908; the publication of *The Masses*, the radical Village journal created in 1910; the Armory Show of 1913, held uptown but championed by Village artists (John Sloan wrote that "the 'new' movements in Art have a rather electrifying effect"); and the innovative Provincetown Playhouse in 1916, which looked for playwrights "capable of bringing down fire from the heavens to the stage."

By 1918, the peak of the next legendary period, Greenwich Village was ablaze with creativity and its consequences. That was the time when John Reed was writing *Ten Days That Shook the World*, Willa Cather published *My Antonia*, and *The Little Review* on West 8th Street serialized James Joyce's *Ulysses* (after four issues, it was closed down for printing "obscene literature").

The Whitney Studio Club opened that year, at 147 West 4th Street. Artist members could "drop by to read or use the ouija board in the library, draw from life or play at billiards, and eventually show their work." Edward Hopper was one of its earliest members, although his first exhibition there was still two years away; in 1918 he was concentrating on etching as he captured New York scenes.

Webster Hall's all-night dances had reached the peak of their popularity by this time, often with two masquerade balls held each week. Originally organized by Villagers as fund-raisers for local radical groups, they were inspired by the 'Quat'z Arts' balls in Paris.

The Provincetown Playhouse moved to its new home at 133 MacDougal Street that November, opening with one-act plays by Eugene O'Neill and Edna St. Vincent Millay. The brand-new moving pictures industry was intrigued enough by bohemian life to build an outdoor studio on Greenwich Avenue and produce the film *A Little Journey to Greenwich Village* in 1918.

That November, Armistice brought the end of World War I. The poet e. e. cummings returned to the Village, along with the demobilized writers John Dos Passos, Malcolm Cowley, and Edmund Wilson.

Sightseers had begun to appear, curious about the goings-on in the Village. By 1918, the Fifth Avenue Coach Company promoted "Bohemian Excursions" that dropped passengers off on Washington Square South with directions to tearooms and art galleries. Even more came by subway, which now connected downtown with the city's transit system, making Sheridan Square the new hub of the Village.

So many tourists came, in fact, that commercial success threatened to overwhelm the literary and artistic life of the Village. By 1927, a headline in the *Christian Science Monitor* read:

(Above) Detail: *Artists' Reception at the Tenth Street Studios,* published in *Frank Leslie's Illustrated Newspaper,* January 23, 1869. The Museum of the City of New York

GREENWICH VILLAGE TOO COSTLY NOW FOR ARTISTS TO LIVE THERE: VALUES INCREASE SO THAT ONLY THOSE WHO CAN WRITE FLUENTLY IN CHECK BOOKS CAN AFFORD IT: ONE ROOM AND BATH COST $65.

Just as there was the cyclical resurgence of creativity in Greenwich Village, there would be the ongoing refrain that the area was finished as a creative center. In the late 1920s, the literary critic Lionel Trilling observed that "I was under no illusion that the Village was any longer in its great days . . . still, the Village was the Village. There seemed no other place in New York where a right-thinking person might live."

During the 1930s, life was defined by the Depression and its economic calamities. By 1934, the concept of public works was expanded to include artists and writers—and many Villagers would not have been able to continue painting or writing without this support. They complained about the many rules and regulations of the WPA: having to report to an office uptown and punch

a time clock, or having to produce a painting within an allotted time (a 16 x 20 canvas had to be completed in four weeks, a water-color in three weeks).

However, since WPA projects paid $23.86 a week and gave free art supplies to full-time painters in 1935 (when few art sales were being made), there were many who were willing to participate—including Jackson Pollock, who worked for the WPA for eight years. A number of other painters who were part

(Above) Jessie Tarbox Beals. *Adele Kennedy, the Village Guide*. c. 1910–17. Photograph. Howard Greenberg Gallery, New York

of this project—Mark Rothko, Ad Reinhardt, and Adolph Gottlieb—would later become known as the New York School in the mid-1940s. By then the Depression was over, World War II had just ended, and another influx of artists and writers had arrived in Greenwich Village.

🌷 🌷 🌷 🌷 🌷

"The Village was as close in 1946 as it would ever come to Paris in the twenties. Rents were cheap, restaurants were cheap, and it seemed to me that happiness itself might be cheaply had. The streets and bars were full of writers and painters and the kind of young men and women who liked to be around them. In Washington Square would-be novelists and poets tossed a football near the fountain and girls just out of Ivy League colleges looked at the landscape with art history in their eyes. People on the benches held books in their hands."

—Anatole Broyard, *Kafka Was the Rage*

An explosion of creativity was taking place in the Village in the late 1940s. Young artists were painting what was just beginning to be known as abstract expressionism, a term coined at the same time as the "New York School" and used interchangeably.

(Left) Hanging a poster for the Greenwich Village Halloween Carnival. 1920s. New York Bound Archives

Young writers were talking about "the New Vision," although by then Jack Kerouac had introduced the word "Beat" to define the attitude of those rebelling against the literary establishment.

Early in 1949, Kerouac headed west on a cross-country trip with friends, traveling at breakneck speed in an unheated car. That spring he would begin writing an account of this adventure, which would finally be published eight years later as the epic *On the Road*—inspiring a generation's pilgrimage to the East Village.

Countless writers (and readers) interested in poetry and the Beats were drawn to the Eighth Street Bookshop (first at 32 West 8th and later across the street at #17). It was opened in 1947 by the Wilentz brothers, Ted and Eli, who

were known for their generosity to many writers—including Allen Ginsberg, who lived above the bookstore for a while. Ginsberg was a key figure in the Beat movement, along with William Burroughs, Gregory Corso, and, of course, Jack Kerouac. At the time, most of the literary coterie scorned Ginsberg and the rest of the Beats as "know nothings."

Artists had just begun to be noticed by the mass media. Jackson Pollock was featured in *Life* magazine in August 1949, with a headline asking, "Is he the greatest living painter in the United States?" The next year, *The New York Herald Tribune* covered the story of eighteen abstract expressionist painters, most of them Villagers, who had mounted a protest against the Metropolitan Museum of Art's juried exhibition. The controversy raged on in other publications and the eighteen artists became known as the Irascibles.

What would become the most important avant-garde artists' organization of that time—the Club—was started in 1949 in a rented loft at 39 East 8th Street. Created as a forum for discussions about modern art, the Club organized famous lecture series open to artists, as well as curators, art critics, collectors, and dealers. They exchanged ideas about art, drank liquor out of tiny paper cups, gave each other tips on available studios, and pushed away the folding chairs to create a dance floor after the evening's lecture.

Over on West 8th Street, in a second floor space, the aesthetics of modernism were being explained by Hans Hofmann, an important teacher of modern art. A young artist could enroll in Hofmann's school, encounter Franz Kline or Willem de Kooning at the Cedar Tavern on almost any night, and attend the Club's lectures on art—all of this within a two-block radius.

The dark and smoky San Remo bar on MacDougal Street was the downtown literary hangout at that time. Frank O'Hara, part of the "New York School of Poets" that often collaborated with the abstract painters, liked to say that he and the other poets divided their time "between the literary bar, the San Remo, and the artists' bar, the Cedar Tavern. In the San Remo we argued and gossiped: in the Cedar we often wrote poems while listening to the painters argue and gossip."

Poets and painters would continue to meet and mingle during the 1950s at Friday night openings in the art galleries on East 10th

Street, at folk concerts in Washington Park, and at the improvised performances known as "Happenings" on St. Mark's Place. The avant-garde Living Theatre performed Gertrude Stein's *Doctor Faustus Lights the Lights* at the Cherry Lane and poetry readings could be heard nightly at the new coffeehouses on MacDougal Street. Thelonius Monk was playing jazz at the Five Spot on Cooper Square and Edward Albee was writing *The Zoo Story* in a tenement on West 4th Street. *The Village Voice* was launched in 1955, at exactly the right moment, a poet noted, "to chronicle the last great flowering of Village bohemianism."

By then the Beats were celebrities and many of the abstract expressionist artists had achieved recognition and financial success (in 1955, *Fortune* magazine listed "speculative" or "growth" painters as investments—including Pollock, de Kooning, and Kline). The younger generation of writers and artists had moved to what became known as the East Village, in search of cheap rents and a more unconventional lifestyle. Greenwich Village began to be inundated with "weekend beatniks," whose attitude was summed up by a poet: "Let's play bohemian, and wear odd clothes, and grow a beard or a ponytail, live in the Village for $200 a month for one small pad and stroll through Washington Square Park with a guitar and a chick looking sad." Hordes of sightseers were back, just as in the earlier decades, and old-timers (and even recent arrivals) lamented that the Village was not the place it once had been.

Bohemia may have left Greenwich Village, but what's left is the beguiling memory of all the creativity that took place here during the century from the 1850s to the 1950s, and the persistent fantasy that it may happen again.

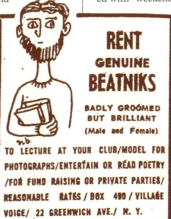

RENT GENUINE BEATNIKS

BADLY GROOMED BUT BRILLIANT (Male and Female)

n.b. TO LECTURE AT YOUR CLUB/MODEL FOR PHOTOGRAPHS/ENTERTAIN OR READ POETRY /FOR FUND RAISING OR PRIVATE PARTIES/ REASONABLE RATES / BOX 490 / VILLAGE VOICE/ 22 GREENWICH AVE./ N. Y.

(Above) Advertisement in *The Village Voice.* **1959**

Map Legend: Walk One

= Structure No Longer Exists

Washington Arch engraving.
The New-York Historical Society

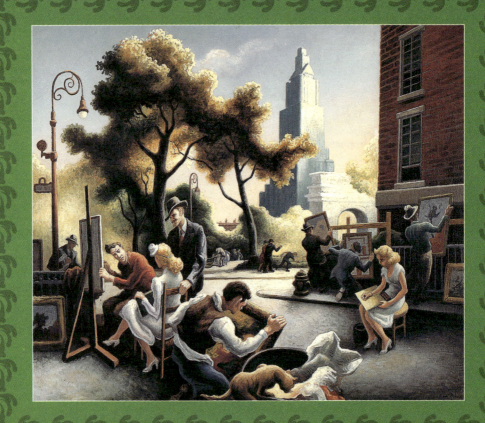

Walk One:

AROUND WASHINGTON SQUARE

"This portion of New York appears to many people the most delectable. It has a kind of established repose which is not of frequent occurrence in other quarters of the long, shrill city; it has a riper, richer, more honorable look . . . the look of having had something of a history."

—Henry James, *Washington Square*

Washington Square has meant so much in stories and myths that we half expect to find the park burgeoning with artists and writers.

There's Eugene O'Neill ambling over to the Provincetown Playhouse, a block away on MacDougal Street. Here's John Reed rushing by, on his way to a raucous evening at the Brevoort (where he'll argue about the Russian Revolution over French wine).

Stanford White is striding along with the blueprints for the design of his Washington Square Arch. And there's Marcel Duchamp sitting on top of the Arch, ready to proclaim Greenwich Village an "Independent Republic."

John Sloan is at one end of the park painting the radiant *Washington Square, Wet Night,* and Berenice Abbott is at the other end photographing The Row, the aristocratic houses scarcely changed through the decades. A stone's throw away, Edgar Allan Poe is tinkering with the final revision of his famous poem "The Raven."

Here's e. e. cummings strolling over from Patchin Place, just as he did every day, to sketch under a crab-apple tree in the park. There's Djuna Barnes, acerbic and pithy, capturing the disso-

(Opposite) Thomas Hart Benton. *The Artists' Show, Washington Square Park.* 1946. Herbert F. Johnson Museum of Art, Cornell University.
(Above) Alexandra Stonehill. Photograph of 80 Washington Square East (detail)

above his studio, Edward Hopper created watercolor compositions of the skylights and chimneys visible from there—geometric patterns of dark forms against a clear sky.

And always, everywhere in Washington Square, there is Henry James. It was here that his grandmother lived "in venerable solitude" on Washington Square North in a house long since demolished. He took his first walks here, "following the nursery-maid with unequal steps." His first school was here, kept by an old lady "who was always having tea in a blue cup, with a saucer that didn't match," where he remembered having enlarged the circle of his observations.

James was born in 1843 at 21 Washington Place, around the corner from the Square. He lived here only six months and then the family moved to Europe, returning when the future writer was four years old. Until he was twelve, he lived at 58 West 14th Street—where there were so many literary visitors from Boston that the guestroom was known permanently as Mr. Emerson's.

nance of the park's patrician north side and the raffish south side in her comment "Satin and motorcars on this side, squalor and push carts on that."

Ringed around the Square, like long ago, are painter's studios, perched high under the eaves to catch the light that floats above the park's treetops. This is where Maurice Prendergast painted his luminous views of lower Fifth Avenue. And climbing to the roof

(Above) Washington Square. c. 1900. New York Bound Archives

For the rest of his life James lived in Europe, recalling New York afternoons in waning summers and remembering a way of life that had long since vanished. His last visit to New York was in 1904, when he stayed with Edith Wharton's sister-in-law Minnie Jones at 21 East 11th Street. Somewhat cranky about all of the changes that had taken place since his boyhood, James dismissed the monument in Washington Square as only "a lamentable little Arch of Triumph." And he was distraught to find that the house where he'd been born "had vanished from the earth, and vanished with it the two or three adjacent houses."

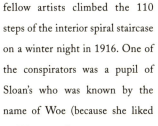

Henry James gave the name Washington Square to one of his best-loved books. He wrote this in the late 1870s but the story takes place four decades earlier, the time of his childhood in New York when the handsome, wide-fronted houses on the Square were still considered modern. Although originally intended to be a short story, it evolved into six installments in *Harper's*—perfectly evoking old New York and its parties, its marriages, its Sunday dinners, and its rigid manners.

🐦 🐦 🐦 🐦 🐦

The top of Washington Square Arch was the scene of a rowdy mock revolution when John Sloan, Marcel Duchamp, and four fellow artists climbed the 110 steps of the interior spiral staircase on a winter night in 1916. One of the conspirators was a pupil of Sloan's who was known by the name of Woe (because she liked the idea of being able to claim "Woe is me").

They carried up Chinese lanterns, red balloons, a supply of candles, and some food and drink. Once they reached the top, they perched on hot-water bottles (it *was* January!) and recited poems, fired cap pistols, and announced that Greenwich Village was now the "Free and Independent Republic of Washington Square."

(Above) *The Quill.* 1923

Three Washington Square North: Edward Hopper used to carry coal scuttles up four flights of stairs here, a climb of seventy-four steps, to heat the old-fashioned potbelly stove in his studio. The house—part of The Row, a series of elegant Greek Revival houses built in the 1830s—was run-down by the time the artist moved in, but its large skylights made up for the lack of heat.

Hopper lived here for fifty-four years (1913–67), a period that spanned a revolution in art styles—although his vision and style remained constant. "The only real influence I've ever had," he once said, "was myself."

He had lived in Paris as a young man but even there he painted on his own, rather than attend art school, and assiduously "avoided Bohemia." When he arrived in Greenwich Village, he liked to attend the sketch class at the Whitney Studio Club and to walk through the Village in the evenings, observing the lights and shadows of the

city. But he never participated in the raffish life of bohemian Greenwich Village.

Hopper seemed to be a confirmed bachelor until he was forty-one, when he married the artist Jo Nivison—who brought along her cat Arthur (known as "the scourge of 9th Street") and her own artistic ambitions. When they took over the entire fourth floor at No. 3, Jo used the north half as her studio and Edward used the south half with the open view of the park.

Greenwich Village is depicted over and over again in Hopper's paintings: *Early Sunday Morning* was originally titled *Seventh Avenue Shops; Nighthawks* was "suggested by a restaurant on Greenwich Avenue where two streets meet"; *November, Washington Square* was the view from his studio, looking across the park.

Sparing of words, famous for his monumental silences, Hopper preferred to let others analyze his paintings. He once remarked that "if you could say it in words, there'd be no reason to paint."

VANISHED FROM THE VILLAGE: TWELVE PICASSOS

The first collection in America that was devoted exclusively to modern art opened in 1927 (two years before The Museum of Modern Art) as the Gallery of Living Art on the ground floor at 100 Washington Square East, in the space now used by the Grey Gallery. Created by Albert Gallatin (the great-grandson of New York University's founder), the collection included twelve Picassos, as well as paintings by Braque, Leger, Juan Gris, Man Ray, Miró, Mondrian, and other modernists. Although this was an important resource for artists, Gallatin was notified by the university in December 1942 that "all nonessentials were to be discontinued during the war years" and the museum's space would have to be vacated. The next month, the entire collection—more than 160 works of art—was given to the Philadelphia Museum of Art.

Today, NYU's Grey Art Gallery presents distinguished art exhibitions throughout the year.

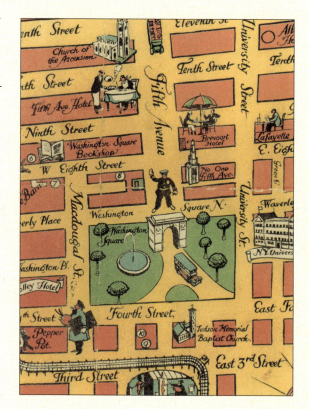

(Right) Tony Sarg. Map of Greenwich Village. 1934. Map Division, The New York Public Library, Astor, Lenox and Tilden Foundations

Many painters lived at Three Washington Square North over the years, including Thomas Eakins, William Glackens, Abbott Thayer, and Rockwell Kent. In the early 1920s, John Dos Passos moved there into a first floor studio where he painted and worked on his novel *Manhattan Transfer*. When both Hopper and Dos Passos had exhibitions at the Whitney Studio Club in 1923, the more unconventional Dos Passos scribbled on his invitations "Come and bring a lot of drunks."

Behind the row of houses on the north side of the Square is picturesque Washington Mews, which had been known as Stable Alley until the stables were converted to skylit studios.

80 Washington Square East was known as "The Benedick" because it was built as an exclusive apartment house for bachelors (Benedick was the confirmed bachelor in *Much Ado About Nothing*). Completed in 1879, this redbrick building was designed

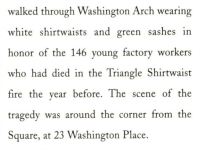

with exotic bohemian apartments for its artistic tenants—including the painter Albert Pinkham Ryder and the poet Wallace Stevens. It was at "The Benedict" that Lily Bart began her downfall in Edith Wharton's *The House of Mirth*.

In the Labor Day parade of 1912, many young women walked through Washington Arch wearing white shirtwaists and green sashes in honor of the 146 young factory workers who had died in the Triangle Shirtwaist fire the year before. The scene of the tragedy was around the corner from the Square, at 23 Washington Place.

42 Washington Square South (since demolished): this was one of those Village rooming houses where "nobody questions your morals, and nobody asks for the rent," wrote John Reed, the writer and political activist who rented one of its back rooms, along with, as he said, "Inglorious Miltons by the Score/ And Rodins, one to every floor."

(Above) Labor Day Parade. 1912. New York Bound Archives

He moved to Greenwich Village in 1912 with three Harvard friends (it is said that waiters at the Brevoort turned pale when the boisterous quartet came for dinner). Captivated by the Village's independent spirit, Reed scribbled a set of rollicking verses titled *The Day in Bohemia: or Life Among the Artists in Manhattan's Quartier Latin.*

Yet we are free who live in Washington Square,
We dare to think as Uptown wouldn't dare,
Blazing our nights with arguments uproarious;
What care we for a dull world censorious
When each is sure he'll fashion something glorious?

John Reed seemed destined for glorious deeds. Exuberant, immensely attractive, wildly energetic, he was an idealist who was divided between being a poet or a revolutionary.

The year after he had arrived in the Village, he became involved in the silk mills strike in Patterson, New Jersey and was sentenced to jail. Once he was released, Reed wrote what became known as the *War in Paterson* story, a legend in American journalism. Working with Mabel Dodge, he then organized the strikers and their families in an extraordinary pageant at Madison Square Garden. While he wrote the script and directed the cast of 2,000, she paid the bills for the production. A few days after the pageant had been triumphantly staged, John Reed and Mabel Dodge, now lovers, sailed to Italy.

(Above) *John Reed*. **c. 1916. Culver Pictures**

SOUTH SIDE OF THE SQUARE

From a bohemian point of view, this was the most interesting stretch of Washington Square. Originally lined with distinguished residences, most of the downtown side had been converted to inexpensive boarding houses and hotels by the beginning of the twentieth century. The most famous of these was 61 Washington Square, which was acclaimed as the "House of Genius" because of its many creative lodgers—including Stephen Crain, Theodore Dreiser, Frank Norris, Alan Seeger, and O. Henry. The house was demolished in 1948 and is now the site of the NYU student union.

Next door, on the corner of Thompson Street, stood a small ramshackle building known as The Garret, a center of Bohemian activity from 1914 until 1926 when it was demolished. Guido Bruno organized poetry readings and published literary book-

lets here in its first years; later it was transformed into a restaurant by Grace Godwin, who served spaghetti to local artists and writers.

At 55 Washington Square, in the next block, is the 1892 Judson Memorial Church designed by Stanford White. The tower and annex adjacent to the church were originally a hotel, with inexpensive studios and living quarters for artists. John Sloan had a studio here for nine years, next door to the impressionist painter Maurice Prendergast.

The buildings on the next block, between MacDougal and Sullivan Streets, were leased by Albert Strunsky, who was known as the Village's "kindliest landlord," always ready to help any artist. "If you needed a place, you would go to him. He always had an empty room," said one Villager. Eventually he lost these buildings because he didn't collect enough of the rents. NYU'S Law School is now located on this site.

There would be other stormy affairs and other involvements in rebel causes for Reed (including his heroic newspaper reports of the war in Mexico), but his two great passions were the Russian Revolution and Louise Bryant. He wrote to a friend that he had "fallen in love again . . . and I think I've found her at last. She's wild and brave and straight, and graceful and lovely to look at." Louise Bryant would in turn assert: "I always wanted somebody who wouldn't care what hour you went to bed or what hour you got up, and who lived in the way Jack did." She left her husband, a dentist in Oregon, and joined Reed in Greenwich Village.

Restless, determined to cover the Russian Revolution, they traveled to the war front and met with Lenin and Trotsky. Returning to Greenwich Village's Patchin Place, each wrote books about their experiences. John Reed's account became the epic *Ten Days That Shook the World*, completed in three months of inspired writing.

Reed later returned to Russia—and died in Moscow, of typhus, when he was thirty-two years old, with Louise Bryant at his side.

He was buried under the walls of the Kremlin, next to other revolutionary heroes.

A year or two earlier, Reed had encountered Sherwood Anderson while they both were hurrying down Ninth Street. They stopped to talk about whether a poet could accomplish more by observing or by fighting to make a better world. Reed was torn but ended the conversation by saying, "Well, somebody has to do the fighting."

BEYOND THE SQUARE

Provincetown Playhouse at 133 MacDougal Street: Eugene O'Neill was twenty-eight years old, with a trunk full of plays, when his first work was staged at the Provincetown Playhouse in 1916. He had worked as a seaman on a tramp steamer, an actor in a touring company, a reporter on a morning newspaper, and a gold prospector in the Spanish Honduras—the quintessential romantic figure, who mistrusted the self-conscious bohemianism of some of the Village's writers and artists.

He had arrived in Greenwich Village straight from Professor George Baker's Playwriting Workshop at Harvard. His father, the famous actor James O'Neill, provided him with a $10-a-week allowance, enough to rent an apartment at 38 Washington Square West.

O'Neill could often be found at the Golden Swan, a ramshackle saloon better known as the Hell Hole, around the corner from the Province-town Playhouse. He felt at home here, drinking with the gangsters and gamblers, the truck drivers and ex-politicians. "They manage to get drunk by hook or crook and keep their pipe dreams," he said, "and that's all they ask of life. I've never known more contented men."

O'Neill found plenty of material for his plays in the Hell Hole, whose habitues were proud of being misfits and tough guys.

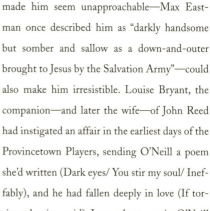

This Irish tavern, with its cheap prints of racehorses and sawdust-covered floor, would later be immortalized as Harry Hope's saloon in *The Iceman Cometh*.

Women loved O'Neill. The moroseness and reserve that made him seem unapproachable—Max East-man once described him as "darkly handsome but somber and sallow as a down-and-outer brought to Jesus by the Salvation Army"—could also make him irresistible. Louise Bryant, the companion—and later the wife—of John Reed had instigated an affair in the earliest days of the Provincetown Players, sending O'Neill a poem she'd written (Dark eyes/ You stir my soul/ Inef-fably), and he had fallen deeply in love (If tor-ture is love, as a wit at the time said). Intensely romantic, O'Neill tended to idealize women, and years later would portray Louise Bryant as the passionate heroine who gets everything she wants, but at a terrible price, in his play *Strange Interlude*.

(Above) Alexandra Stonehill. Photograph of Village Mews house

Eugene O'Neill and the Provincetown Playhouse were inextricably linked, since the depth and power of O'Neill's plays created the early success of this new theater on MacDougal Street. Its small company had started with a subscription list of sixty-four names and a dream of producing American plays of artistic and dramatic merit. By 1925, in less than ten years, the Provincetown Players had produced ninety-three new plays and inspired such enthusiasm for drama that there were 1,900 "little theaters" throughout the country.

135-137 MacDougal Street: Three of the Village's liveliest ventures were once located here. The Liberal Club, founded in 1913 as a "Meeting Place for Those Interested in New Ideas," was upstairs in two large parlors and a sunroom at 137; downstairs, in the basement, Polly's Restaurant offered easy credit and homey meals in a cozy space with yellow walls. Next door, at 135, the Washington Square Bookshop was nicknamed the Village Pump, known as the place to come for local gossip, radical literature, and "all the books the regular booksellers did not care to handle."

These three places were so intertwined that they became a rendezvous for many Villagers. On Friday nights, the Liberal Club charged 25¢ for wine-and-talk parties, or to dance to the music of the player piano, and patrons often ended the evening downstairs at Polly's swinging to the new ragtime dances. Eventually a wall was broken down between the Bookshop and the Liberal Club to create a space large enough for lectures and to encourage book browsing, but the neighborhood

(Above) Jessie Tarbox Beals. *Polly Holladay's Restaurant*. c. 1917. Photograph. Howard Greenberg Gallery, New York

WINING AND DINING IN GREENWICH VILLAGE

"In all the typical Greenwich Village restaurants
you will find the same elusive something, the spirit of
the picturesque, the untrammelled, the quaint and
charming—in short, the different!"

—Anna Alice Chapin, Greenwich Village *(1917)*

Even in the early decades of the twentieth century, Greenwich Village was known for its abundance of small charming restaurants, lively cafes, cozy bars, and tucked-away clubs and cabarets. Many of these were peripatetic ventures: two of the best known places—Polly's and Romany Marie's—each had three or four Village addresses, always with an artistic decor. Stuart Davis painted the sign for Polly Holladay's restaurant at Sheridan Square and Buckminster Fuller decorated Romany Marie's West 8th Street tearoom.

There were at least 45 tearooms in the Village in the 1920s. These bohemian places often had names that were vaguely Left Bank, such as the Garret, La Boheme, the Crumperie, or were exuberantly colorful, like the Black Parrot, Purple Pup, Blue Horse, or Red Head (renamed "21" when it moved uptown to 52nd Street).

During Prohibition, Greenwich Village was known as one of the easiest places in New York to get a drink. The most famous of its speakeasies was Barney Gallant's Speako De Luxe, which served cocktails at 19 Washington Square North. Nightlife in Greenwich Village was lively in the cabarets and clubs--and perhaps the liveliest place of all was Café Society, a racially integrated nightclub at 2 Sheridan Square, where boogie-woogie pianists and Billie Holiday performed during the 1930s and '40s.

bohemians tended to use the bookstore as a lending library and to consider Polly's Restaurant as their private dining annex.

Polly's contentious cook-and-waiter Hippolyte Havel—an avowed anarchist who would sometimes snarl *Bourgeois pigs!* as he served the customers—was once asked by a tourist to define the boundaries of Greenwich Village. Enraged, he replied "Greenwich Village is a state of mind—it has no boundaries."

HANG-OUTS

Both the Minetta and the San Remo—literary drinking places on MacDougal Street—were closely identified with Maxwell Bodenheim in his later years. This colorful bohemian poet (who was said to resemble the movie idol Rudolf Valentino) arrived in Greenwich Village in the 1920s and immediately began to create legends about himself. He became known as *The Great Lover of the Village*, incessantly pursued by fawning young girls. Every newspaper in the country followed the story when two of these girls committed suicide (one of them distraught because he'd called her poetry "sentimental slush") but Bodenheim reveled in the notoriety. By the 1950s, this picturesque eccentric had become a pathetic drunk, sleeping on park benches and scribbling his poems on scraps of paper in exchange for a drink in a Village hangout. He was murdered in a Bowery flophouse in 1954.

Bodenheim's best line was the often-repeated epigram that "Greenwich Village is the Coney Island of the soul."

(Above) Jessie Tarbox Beals. Washington Square Book Shop. c. 1910–17. Photograph. Howard Greenberg Gallery, New York

113 MacDougal Street: Minetta Tavern was where you would find the Beat writers Allen Ginsburg, Jack Kerouac, and Gregory Corso, as well as the eccentric bohemian Joe Gould, who claimed to speak the language of seagulls.

The back room of the Minetta still has 1930s murals of the Village, but the valuable sketches—those by Franz Kline—were sold long ago.

93 MacDougal Street: site of the San Remo bar, a hangout for intellectual hipsters during the 1940s and 1950s (after a night of martinis, marijuana, and arguments about existentialism, it was sometimes called the San Remorse). A Villager remembers that "the Remo was where it was all happening then—for Styron, Kerouac, Broyard, and a hundred other writers . . . it was the international communications center for the young and hungry literati. Everyone there was trying to accumulate a few hundred dollars to get to Europe—as in Hemingway's earlier days—and the Remo was the last stop before boarding the Holland-American Line in Hoboken, and the first stop on the return."

Coffeehouses in the Neighborhood:

Caffe Reggio at 119 MacDougal is still the classic Italian coffeehouse, with tiny tables and a gigantic brass espresso machine; it's also the oldest in the Village, open since 1927.

Other venerable coffeehouses are Le Figaro, on the corner of MacDougal and Bleecker Streets, and Caffe Dante, down the street at 81 MacDougal.

(Above) Jessie Tarbox Beals. *Minetta Lane*. c. 1910. Photograph. Howard Greenberg Gallery, New York

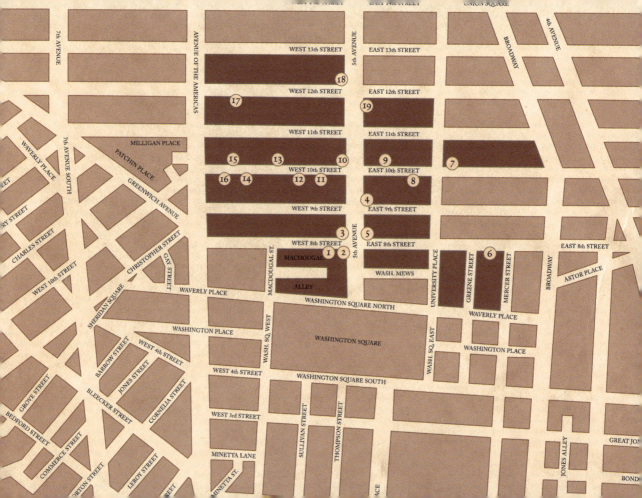

Map Legend: Walk Two

1. 8 West 8th Street: site of The Whitney Museum of American Art, now the New York Studio School
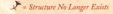 2. SW corner of Fifth Avenue and 8th Street: site of The Marble House
3. 10 Fifth Avenue: Thimble Theater
 4. 23 Fifth Avenue: site of Mabel Dodge's salon
 5. NE Corner of Fifth Avenue and 8th Street: site of the Brevoort Hotel
 6. 46 East 8th Street: site of Jackson Pollock's studio
7. 23 East 10th Street: The Albert
8. 16 East 10th Street: The Pen and Brush Club
9. 9 East 10th Street: Dawn Powell's home
10. NW corner of Fifth Avenue and 10th Street: Church of the Ascension
11. 14 West 10th Street: Mark Twain's home
12. 28 West 10th Street: Marcel Duchamp's home
13. 37 West 10th Street: Sinclair Lewis and Dorothy Thompson's home
14. 54 West 10th Street: Hart Crane's home
 15. 51 West 10th Street: site of the Tenth Street Studio
 16. 58 West 10th Street: site of the Tile Club
17. 66 West 12th Street: The New School University
18. 60 Fifth Avenue: Forbes Building, originally the Macmillan Company
19. 47 Fifth Avenue: Salmagundi Club

 = Structure No Longer Exists

Jessie Tarbox Beals. *The Village Guide.* c. 1917.
Photograph. Howard Greenberg Gallery, New York

LOWER FIFTH AVENUE

8 West 8th Street: Gertrude Vanderbilt Whitney founded The Whitney Museum of American Art here in 1931. She had arrived in Greenwich Village decades before, when she remodeled a MacDougal Alley stable into a sculpture studio for

herself. Although she continued to live uptown in a house with fifty-four rooms, Gertrude Whitney was thrilled with her new studio, noting that "the ceiling is high and one's ideas soar upward. I felt at once that I must do something large in it."

There was always a dichotomy between her immense wealth, with all of its obligations, and her work as a serious artist—and in an extraordinary way, she combined these two parts of her life to become a patron of other artists. John Sloan wrote that "No

one will ever know the extent of the private benefactions Mrs. Whitney performed . . . I know of innumerable artists whose studio rent was paid, or pictures purchased just at the right time to keep the wolf from the door, or hospital expenses paid, or a trip to Europe made possible."

Gertrude Whitney's support of American artists had begun at the 1908 exhibition of rebellious artists, known as "The Eight." She purchased four paintings, despite the ferocious public response to the exhibit. "At that time," an artist would later observe, "to buy such unfashionable pictures was almost as revolutionary as painting them."

She decided to create a gallery—the Whitney Studio, at 8 West 8th Street—in which American artists could congregate and

(Opposite) Robert Henri. *Gertrude Vanderbilt Whitney.* 1916. Whitney Museum of American Art
(Above) Jessie Tarbox Beals. *MacDougal Alley.* c. 1916-17. Photograph. Howard Greenberg Gallery, New York

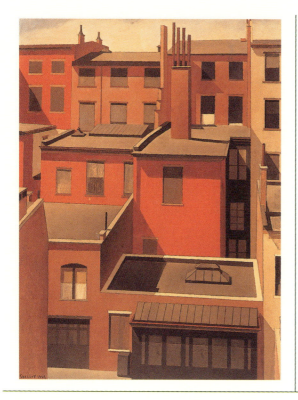

show their work. The Whitney Studio Club came soon after, at 147 West 4th Street, with exhibition space, a library filled with new art books, a squash court in the backyard, and studio space on the top floor for the sketch classes (admission was 20¢ per session, with professional models).

Over the years Gertrude Whitney would acquire four adjoining brownstones on 8th Street and join them together to create the Whitney Museum, with a rapidly expanding collection of American art. Appropriately, the building now houses an acclaimed art school—the New York Studio School—that teaches drawing, painting, sculpture, and art history, with exhibitions and evening lectures open to the public.

A visit to Gertrude Whitney's studio was described by the sculptor Daniel Chester French, who lived nearby: *"Mrs. Whitney called me up the other day and asked me to come in and see her statue. . . . She herself was more striking than the statue, in a gown of orange and dark blue flowered stripes, brilliant beyond reason. With her dark hair and white skin and crimson lips, she was by far the brightest thing on the landscape."*

(Above) Charles Sheeler. *MacDougal Alley*. 1924. Davison Art Center, Wesleyan University

Picturesque, cobble-stoned MacDougal Alley was nicknamed "Alley de Luxe" after artists began creating studios out of the old livery stables. Tenants included the sculptors Daniel Chester French and Isamu Noguchi.

Southwest corner of 8th Street and Fifth Avenue: the city's first important collection of paintings belonged to John Taylor Johnston, railroader and art patron, who lived here in what was known as the Marble House. The paintings were hung in a private gallery above his stable on 8th Street and were shown to the public on Thursday afternoons. Johnston later gave much of his collection to the Metropolitan Museum.

Northwest corner of 8th Street and Fifth Avenue: 10 Fifth Avenue, which still exists, once housed the Thimble Theatre on the second floor. This tiny playhouse was created by Charles Edison—poet and son of the inventor—who collaborated with the eccentric Village publisher Guido Bruno to organize a theater group in 1916, performing Chekov, Gogol, and the first American production of Strindberg's *Miss Julie.* The theater lasted for just one season.

(Above) Fifth Avenue and West 8th Street. 1911. New York Bound Archives

PETITS JOURNAUX OR LITTLE MAGAZINES

Nearly twenty small publications had a Greenwich Village address in the early years of the twentieth century. These journals tended to be very opinionated, sharply provocative, independently financed—and often short-lived. Their direction was either political (ranging from a socialist point of view to out-right anarchy) or literary (publishing avant-garde poetry and criticism).

The best known of the political publications was The Masses, *whose editorial offices were at 91 Greenwich Avenue. The masthead proclaimed its role to be "frank, arrogant, impertinent, searching for true causes; a magazine whose final policy is to do as it pleases and conciliate nobody, not even its readers." With Max Eastman as its feisty editor,* The Masses *published radical opinions*

for four years until the government forced it to close in 1917, when it campaigned against American involvement in World War I.

The next year, an undaunted Eastman started a new magazine called The Liberator—*with offices at 138 West 13th Street. Its premiere issue published John Reed's firsthand account of the Russian Revolution. In 1934, a radical quarterly was launched by the left-wing John Reed Club; this was the* Partisan Review, *which eventually declared its independence from any political group and went on to become a major literary journal. It, too, had a Village address, at 45 Astor Place.*

The literary journals published in Greenwich Village from 1915 through the 1920s consciously promoted the newest cultural movements: imagist poetry, feminism, modern art, symbolism, and Freudian analysis. Some publications were of major critical importance and read internationally, such as the "experimental and unconventional" Dial, at 152 West 13th Street, which first published T. S. Eliot's "The Waste Land." The little Quill, conversely, was a local humor magazine with inane gossip and clumsy verse. Several publications moved to the Village from other places: Broom arrived from Europe and settled in at 3 East 9th Street, while The Little Review moved from Chicago to a basement office at 31 West 14th Street and then on to 27 West 8th Street, serializing James Joyce's Ulysses beginning in the March 1918 issue. The many Bruno publications were a conglomeration of neighborhood news and the occasion gem—Hart Crane's first poem was published in Bruno's Bohemia in 1917. Many journals lasted only for a year or two—including the Ink Pot, the Greenwich Village Spectator, Rogue, Seven Arts— before disappearing into oblivion.

THE FEBRUARY 1915 10 CENTS
MASSES

"A DAUGHTER OF THE REVOLUTION" BY JOHN REED

FRANK WALTS 14

23 Fifth Avenue (since demolished): Before Mabel Dodge created her famous salon at this address, she had designed its perfect setting: a room that was luminously white, with heavy white paper covering the walls, an elaborate white Venetian chandelier, and a white bearskin rug in front of the white marble fireplace.

This restrained and elegant space was filled on Wednesday evenings with a cacophony of noisy talk, while the guests took sides and wrangled over psychoanalysis, birth control, and trade unionism—topics that were taboo in most living rooms in 1912. "Arguments and discussions floated in the air, were caught and twisted and hauled and tied, until the white salon was no longer static. There were undercurrents of emotion and sex," remembered one visitor.

During her salon evenings Mabel Dodge usually sat aloof and withdrawn, while her guests—"poor and rich, labor-skates, scabs, strikers and unemployed, painters, musicians, reporters, editors, swells"—did all the talking.

VIVE LA FRANCE

When Villagers wanted to celebrate (having sold a painting, gotten a book advance, or were off skylarking with friends), they chose to dine superbly at either the Brevoort or the Lafayette. The two hotels were a block apart, with the Brevoort on the corner of Fifth and 8th Street, and the Lafayette on the corner of University Place and 9th Street. Eventually both were owned by Raymond Orteig, who was famous for putting up the $25,000 prize for the first transatlantic airplane flight—won by Charles Lindbergh in 1925.

For a century (from 1854 to 1954), the Brevoort Hotel brought the spirit of *la belle France* to lower Fifth Avenue, with its sidewalk cafe (the first in New York) and its celebrated menu. "Never, this side of Paris, have there been such frog's legs, such *pommes de terre souffles*, such sauce bernaise . . ." raved a 1930s dining guide, adding that it was "little wonder then that truly great plays are written at the tables of the Brevoort, between the *fromage* and the *demitasse;* that true Bohemians, in pursuit of the Muse, have come in for

(Opposite) John Sloan. *The Lafayette*. 1928. The Metropolitan Museum of Art

luncheon and stayed on for dinner." After the all-night balls at Webster Hall, this is where the revelers came to quaff champagne and eat shirred eggs at the famous breakfast parties.

The most talked-about occasion at the Brevoort may have been the night Prohibition became the law, on July 1, 1919. At midnight, waiters were sent downstairs to the wine cellar to haul up the cases of whiskies and wines. These were sold at cost to the habitues, who feared that this might be their last drink. On that night Washington Square Park "echoed as never before to raucous, pagan shrieks" with much wild splashing and nude bathing in the fountain.

The Lafayette was also a favorite of the artistic and literary crowd, who liked the corner cafe with its French menu and its marble-topped tables, green-shaded lamps, tall windows overlooking the street, and corner rack filled with French newspapers.

The writer Dawn Powell held court here, choosing a corner seat where she could observe the various comings and goings. She once lived around the corner from the Lafayette—so close, she said, that she could look out the window and watch as her checks bounced over there.

46 East 8th Street: when Jackson Pollock was living and painting here on the top floor (that building has since been replaced with another), he knocked down a wall so that he would have space to create a monumental twenty-foot mural for Peggy Guggenheim. The stretched canvas wasn't touched for six

(Above) Bernard Schardt. *Jackson Pollock*. 1944. Photograph. Pollock-Krasner House and Study Center, East Hampton, New York

months and then, in January 1944, Pollock painted the mural in one night. "Dancing around the room, he finally found a way of painting that fitted him, and from then on he developed that technique and that scale," another artist wrote. This was the beginning of a new way of painting, which would evolve into Pollock's radical poured or dripped abstractions that exploded the traditions of painting away from the easel.

Pollock had come to New York in 1930 to study at the Art Students League, signing up for classes with the Regionalist painter Thomas Hart Benton. He admired Benton, defended his ideas to the other art students, went to his home at 10 East 8th Street for Sunday night spaghetti dinners, and helped mix paint or clean brushes when Benton worked on the New School murals. Later Pollock would repudiate this influence, claiming that "he drove his kind of realism at me so hard I bounced right into nonobjective painting."

During his early years in Greenwich Village, Pollock struggled to support his painting. He worked as a janitor at the City and Country School on West 13th Street and as a stonecutter cleaning the Peter Cooper statue in Cooper Square. Finally, when the WPA Federal Art Project was formed in 1935, he was chosen as one of the participating artists.

Pollock had moved to 46 East 8th Street in 1935 and remained there for ten years—with his brother Sande for the first seven years, and then with the painter Lee Krasner, who became his wife and strongest supporter. Even after he and Krasner had moved to Springs, at the eastern end of Long Island, in 1945, their connection to Greenwich Village continued. Pollock visited the Fourth Avenue booksellers and bought volumes on Ethnology, studying the lithographs of sand paintings. He and Krasner stayed in a friend's MacDougal Alley studio (where he could show his large paintings) during the winters in the early 1950s. Often, when he came to the city, Pollock

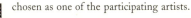

Alexandra Stonehill. Photograph of Webster Hall (detail)

could be found at the Cedar Street Tavern: tormented by depression, he headed here ready to drink and carouse all night with the other artists. He was often belligerent when drunk—and was banned for a spell for kicking in the door to the men's room at the Cedar.

24 University Place, on the corner of 8th Street: the site of the Cedar Street Tavern, the raffish bar where the artists congregated (since demolished, although a bar of the same name is located a few blocks north). Described as drab, with shabby green walls that were bare except for a few Hogarth prints and an industrial clock "whose hands sometimes turned backward like a prop in a Cocteau movie."

In 1957, when Larry Rivers tied for first prize on the quiz show "The $64,000 Challenge" (answering questions about Picasso and Archipenko in the category "Contemporary Art"), he carried his $32,000 check to the Cedar and bought drinks for everyone.

TENTH STREET

23 East 10th Street: The Albert, once a hotel and now an apartment house, was named for the artist Albert Pinkham Ryder,

(Above) Peggy Bacon. *Dawn Powell*. 1934. Drawing. Kraushaar Galleries, New York

whose brother owned the building (Jackson Pollock described Ryder as "the only American artist that interests me"). When Thomas Wolfe was teaching at New York University in the 1920s, he lived in room 2220 of the Hotel Albert.

16 East 10th Street: The Pen and Brush Club, an organization of professional women in the arts—writers, painters, sculptors, musicians—founded in 1892 to promote intellectual camaraderie among women. The public may visit members' exhibitions in the front parlors of this typical Village house.

9 East 10th Street: Dawn Powell, the witty and satirical author best known for her 1940s and '50s novels and plays, lived here for eight years and then moved around the corner to 35 East 9th Street for the next sixteen years. "The Village is my creative oxygen," she wrote in her diary. Page after page of the diary describe her peregrinations to Greenwich Village speakeasies and cafes, which in turn were frequently depicted in her work. *The Wicked Pavilion* is known as her Hotel Lafayette book, just as *The Golden Spur* is called her Cedar Tavern novel. In an October 1949 entry in her diary she recalls meeting a fellow writer in the Lafayette: "No one but you," he said, "is doing for New York what Balzac did for Paris."

When Dawn Powell was sketched by the equally witty and sardonic artist Peggy Bacon, she wrote in her diary that the pastel caricature "looked just like me, depressingly enough." The artist had scribbled her own description at the bottom of one sketch: "Sturdy, robust body like Brueghel roisterer . . . bright satirical shoe button eyes far apart . . . really ribald sophisticate au natural."

The Church of the Ascension, on the Northwest corner of 10th Street and Fifth Avenue, captivated Henry James when he visited New York in 1904. He described entering the church "at noon, and standing for the first time in the presence of that noble work (the altar mural) of John LaFarge . . . the hot light, outside, might have been that of an Italian piazzetta; the cool shade, within, with the important work of art shining through it, seemed part of some other-world pilgrimage."

14 West l0th Street: Mark Twain lived here, but only for a winter. He spent a longer time (1904-1908) at 21 Fifth Avenue (now demolished). Twain's favorite pastime in New York, when he was not playing billiards, was to stroll along Fifth Avenue in his white suit.

28 West 10th: the French artist Marcel Duchamp resided here in the 1960s. A chess master, he used the game as a recurring theme in his work—and often played across the street at the Marshall Chess Club at 23 West 10th Street.

37 West 10th: the home of Sinclair Lewis and Dorothy Thompson, who moved here after their marriage in 1928 when he was the most famous writer in America, after the triumphant success of his novel *Main Street.*

54 West 10th: the poet Hart Crane lived here when he first moved to Greenwich Village in 1917. He could barely afford the

$6 weekly rent, but at least his job on the little journal *Pagan* entitled him to a supply of passes to the Village theaters.

51 West 10th (demolished in 1956): The legendary 1858 Tenth Street Studio was the first building ever designed exclusively for artists, with three floors of well-lit studios and a dramatic glass-domed exhibition hall. Art critics, patrons, and the curious public flocked here to see art—in the early years, the building was described "as full as a Broadway omnibus on a rainy day."

The artists working and living here included some of America's best-known painters and sculptors, but it was William Merritt Chase who was particularly associated with the building. He took over the communal gallery as his studio (very cluttered, with tapestries, Javanese curios, and 37 samovars) and turned it into a luxurious space that he used for exhibitions, art classes, musicales, and lavish parties. With his Russian wolfhounds and red fez,

Chase was the epitome of "a real bohemian . . . just escaped from the Latin Quarter."

58 West 10th: The exclusive Tile Club, famous in the 1880s as a forum for discussing new ideas in art, met in a little garden structure behind the main house. These prominent artists were considered somewhat snobbish bohemians (one artist was heard shouting to the cook that "the soup is a Velasquez").

70 West 10th Street, the Post Office: Joe Gould was often seen here filling his fountain pen, but it's true that he was seen all over the Village from 1917 into the 1950s. He claimed to be writing *An Oral History of the World*, in which he recorded all of the conversations overheard in his wanderings about the city. There were more than eleven million words, he told everyone, with hundreds of thousands of words devoted entirely to the sexual adventures of Greenwich Villagers in the 1920s.

Gould, who was 5 feet 4 inches tall, alleged that the manuscript was 7 feet high, making him "the only author in history who had written a book taller than himself." He carried a battered portfolio around the Village, now and then pulling out the kind of composition book used by schoolchildren and scribbling away. Penniless, he would go from one Village saloon to the next to cadge a drink in exchange for reciting a poem or imitating a seagull.

A graduate of Harvard, he liked to claim that he was the last of the bohemians (adding that the rest of them were dead, in the loony bin, or in the advertising business). Gould tried for ten years to join the Raven Poetry Circle in the Village (this was the group that put on poetry exhibitions in Washington Square every summer) but he was always blackballed. The Ravens let him attend their poetry readings, although they suspected he came only for the wine they served. At one of their Poetry Nights, they were enraged when he recited "My Religion": *In winter I'm a Buddhist / And in summer I'm a nudist.*

Gould was immortalized by Joseph Mitchell—another Villager—who published a profile of him in the *New Yorker* and later wrote the book *Joe Gould's Secret.* Mitchell had guessed, correctly, that the *Oral History of Our Time* didn't exist except in Gould's imagination. He waited until after Gould's death to tell the story, letting him continue to describe his book and its "long-winded conversations and short and snappy conversations, brilliant conversations and foolish conversations . . . shouts in the night, wild rumors, cries from the heart."

66 West 12th Street: The New School University, founded in 1919. The design of this Bauhaus-inspired building caused a sensation when it was built in 1931. Thomas Hart Benton and Jose Clemente Orozco were commissioned to paint interior murals—and the Orozco frecoes are still here, in a seventh floor conference room (open to the public when not in use).

The New School became the "university in exile" for the intelligentsia fleeing Nazi Germany in the 1930s. Its adult education classes are legendary: Tennessee Williams took a course in playwriting here and Jack Kerouac studied Impressionist paintings in Meyer Shapiro's classes.

60 Fifth Avenue, corner of 12th Street: Forbes Building, originally the Macmillan Company. This has been a publishing headquarters ever since this building opened in 1925. Macmillan published books here for four decades; since then Forbes has continued the tradition with its own publications.

47 Fifth Avenue: the Salmagundi Club, founded in 1870. This artists' club was named after the series of high-spirited, audacious pamphlets published by Washington Irving and written in the manner of London's *Spectator.* Today, members' art exhibitions are open to the public.

(Above) Alexandra Stonehill. Photograph of a nineteenth-century book from the Salmagundi Club library

Map Legend: Walk Three

= Structure No Longer Exists

The West Village's winding streets are a joy to wander through, but can turn a walking tour into a circuitous maze. Rather than planning a specific route, it's suggested that walkers amble through these narrow streets that idiosyncratically have names rather than numbers.

THE LAIR OF CLIVETTE IN SHERIDAN SQUARE - GREENWICH VILLAGE -

Jessie Tarbox Beals. *The Lair of Clivette in Sheridan Square.* c. 1910–17. Photograph. Howard Greenberg Gallery, New York

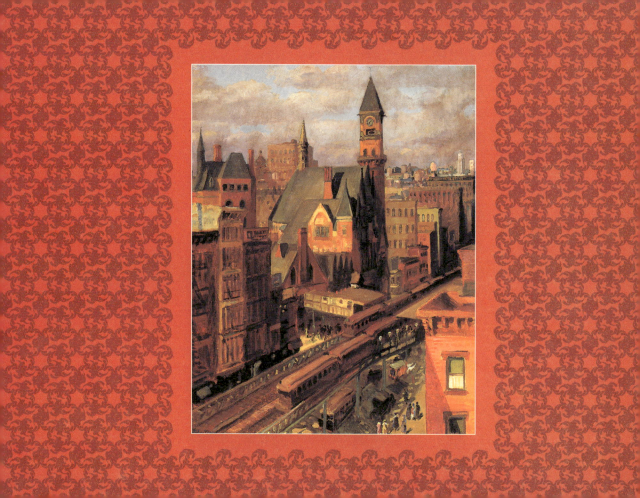

Walk Three:

SHERIDAN SQUARE and the WEST VILLAGE

Art and literature come together with particular gusto at the corner of West Tenth Street and Sixth Avenue: Jefferson Market Library's flamboyant turrets and gables have been captured over and over by Greenwich Village artists, while across the street there are myriad literary associations at Patchin Place, that narrow lane shaded by ailanthus trees.

JEFFERSON MARKET

No artist painted Greenwich Village with as much affection and authenticity as John Sloan. He took the ordinary commonplaces of life and imbued them

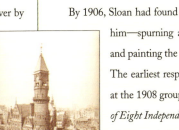

with exuberance and pathos: the crowded Sixth Avenue Elevated careening across a winter sky, scrubwomen in the library at Astor Place, spring planting in a Village backyard, a movie theater on Carmine Street, the murky atmosphere of McSorleys, the choreography of children playing in Washington Square Park.

By 1906, Sloan had found the subject matter that was right for him—spurning academic subjects for raw urban life and painting the city in all its ragtag vigor and squalor. The earliest response from the critics and public was at the 1908 group exhibition, known as the *Exhibition of Eight Independent Painters*—or simply The Eight—whose work had been rejected by the conservative uptown National Academy of Design. Sloan and the other early realists were labeled as rebels, apostles of ugliness, or, that detested label, the Ashcan School.

Most of the painters in this group lived in Greenwich Village, as did Sloan from 1912 to 1935—the same years that he was doc-

(Opposite) John Sloan. *Jefferson Market*. 1917; retouched 1922. The Pennsylvania Academy of the Fine Arts
(Above) Jefferson Market. 1904. New York Bound Archives

umenting the city and its people. He and his wife Dolly moved from 61 Perry Street to 240 West 4th and then to a fifth floor studio facing north at 88 Washington Place, where he painted one of his best-loved works, *Jefferson Market, Sixth Avenue*. This fanciful red-brick 1877 Venetian Gothic building then served as a courthouse and Sloan often stopped by its Night Court, fascinated by the daily tragedy and comedy enacted here ("This is much more stirring to me than the great majority of plays," he wrote in his diary.) His next move was to 53 Washington Square South in the Judson Annex, which he described as a heavenly abode with its fourth-floor view of the park and the Arch. Sloan's marriage to Dolly was intensely complicated but lasted for forty-two years. After her death, he was happily married to Helen Farr, a former pupil of his.

Despite eventual acclaim, Sloan was never able to make a living by his art alone but had to count on income from illustrating and teaching. As a young man, his routine was to take just enough commercial assignments—magazine etchings, book illustrations,

(Above) John Sloan painting on the canvas of *Buses in the Square*. c. 1927. Delaware Art Museum

THE ASHCAN SCHOOL

The artists of the Ashcan School set a bold new direction in American art by painting contemporary life—in the two decades prior to 1917—with a realism that shocked the public. Their subject was everyday life with all its vitality and sometimes sordid chaos: boxing matches, political rallies, crowded tenements, window shoppers, young ruffians fighting a tin can battle, and a myriad of newly-arrived immigrants.

The six major artists of the Ashcan School were John Sloan, Robert Henri, William Glackens, George Luks, Everett Shinn, and George Bellows. Most of them had worked as illustrators for newspapers and magazines before becoming artists, so that their art conveyed the immediacy of an on-the-scene report as they documented the social inequality and ethnic diversity of New York in that era.

Art critics of the time often called painters of the Ashcan School "devotees of the ugly." Yet, rather than deliberately seeking the rowdy and unrefined, these artists believed that beauty could be found in ordinary life. Their work became recognized for its "power to find grace in billboards, idylls in Sixth Avenue, and beauty in everything."

(Above) Alexandra Stonehill. Photograph of artist's palette from the Salmagundi Club collection

posters—to pay the bills, and then to spend the rest of his time painting. His staunchest ally was always the Whitney Museum on 8th Street, which gave him his first one-man show in 1916 and continued to buy his paintings to add to their collection.

Sloan's ferocious idealism may have been best expressed when he was the art editor of *The Masses*, the radical journal that published, as one critic enthused, "those rude, raw drawings of Mr. Sloan and his friends, so different from the insipidities of all other magazines." During one year—1913—he contributed four covers and thirty-two drawings to this journal even though there was no payment for work published. He later admitted "the strange thing was that if I got a good idea, I gave it to *The Masses*. If I got a second-rate one, I might sell it to *Harper's*, but I could never have the same feeling when working for pay."

PATCHIN PLACE

The poet e. e. cummings lived for nearly four decades in Patchin Place—describing it as "a certain diminutive deadend lane of

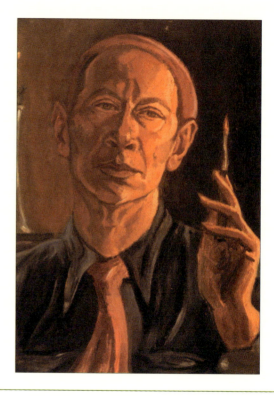

(Above) e. e. cummings. *Self-portrait.* c. 1940. Corbis

hundredyearold houses." He moved to No. 4 in 1924, into a third floor room with good light for painting (in those days he painted more than he wrote, calling himself "an author of pictures, a draughtsman of words") and eventually acquired other floors of the house. His paintings hung on all the available wall space, books thronged the ground floor, and his collection of miniature elephants trekked across the bookcases and mantel. When it was teatime, his wife Marion rang a little elephant bell to call him down from the top floor studio where he was composing poems with a staccato typography that excited readers.

He could dazzle his friends with the intensity of his talk, the "geysers of talk." It must have sounded very like his poetry: "it was comical ironical learned brilliantlycolored intricatelycadenced damnable poetic and sometimes naughty," wrote John Dos Passos, with whom he roamed about the city, walking through the Village or over to Cafe Royale on Second Avenue. Whatever the weather, cummings walked to Washington Square every day to sketch in his black-bound notebook.

Courtly, handsome, an intense listener as well as an eager talker, cummings welcomed the visits of his fellow poets—T. S. Eliot, Dylan Thomas, and Ezra Pound all made a pilgrimage to Patchin Place—but he was diffident towards the young fans who knocked on his door.

Patchin Place was also the home of the writers John Masefield (a porter at a neighborhood bar when he lived here and, much later, poet laureate of England) and John Reed, who lived at No. 1 while he was writing *Ten Days That Shook the World.*

Still another resident was Djuna Barnes, famous for her satirical novel *Nightwood*, who lived in one tiny robin's egg-blue room at 5 Patchin Place. She had been a lively figure in Greenwich Village's literary and lesbian circles in the 1910s, writing plays for the Provincetown Players and publishing acerbic Greenwich Village stories—including "The Last Petit Souper," a tour of bohemian cafes. During her final years she was a recluse, with a "Do Not Disturb" sign fastened to her chartreuse door.

SHERIDAN SQUARE

"I was reflecting the other night meaning I was being reflected upon that Sheridan Square is remarkably beautiful. . . ."

—Frank O'Hara

The center of bohemianism was Sheridan Square, the oldest and most picturesque part of Greenwich Village. Although its rows of small redbrick houses evoked the refinement and order of an ear-

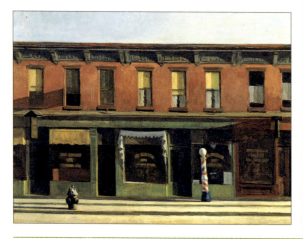

lier century, nevertheless this is where the nonconformists and mavericks flocked—just before and after World War I—to celebrate the avant-garde and to boldly defy respectability.

By then the houses in this neighborhood were often shabby and timeworn, partitioned into many small spaces. The parlors and basements were turned into tearooms or shops with a bohemian decor when tourists began to descend on Greenwich Village. By 1918, Sheridan Square was being described by *Vanity Fair* as an area teeming with "artists, decorators, writers of *vers libre*, scene painters, playwrights, bird stick varnishers and smock designers."

AROUND THE SQUARE:

Even Villagers are confused at this intersection: what seems to be Sheridan Park is actually Christopher Park, with an equestrian statue of the Civil War general Philip Sheridan and a life-sized sculpture of two couples (bronze with a white patina) called *Gay Liberation* by George Segal. The Square was the

(Above) Edward Hopper. *Early Sunday Morning*. 1930. Whitney Museum of American Art

scene of rioting during both the 1863 Civil War Draft Riots and the 1969 Stonewall rebellion, when thousands of gays and lesbians protested police harassment and launched a national gay rights movement.

The Greenwich Village Theatre on Sheridan Square staged the musical revue *Greenwich Village Follies* for two years (1919 and 1920) until the Shuberts whisked this hugely successful satire uptown to Broadway.

A photography gallery and coffeehouse—Limelight—was opened near Sheridan Square at 91 Seventh Avenue South in the 1950s. Inspired by the Paris cafes, Limelight was meant to be a place for photographers to meet each other and to exhibit their work. Helen Gee, its creator, described its early years: "At one table you'd find Philippe Halsman drinking coffee with friends; at another Arnold Newman; Cornell Capa at an eight-seater with a contingent from *Life*; and Weegee, at no table, just roaming around." Imogen Cunningham and Minor White's photographs sold for ten dollars; Robert Franks and

Bill Brandt asked for twenty-five; Berenice Abbott, thirty-five; Eugene Smith and Edward Weston, fifty; and Paul Strand, "a staggering one hundred and twenty-five." The gallery closed in 1961.

45 Grove Street: site of the house where Thomas Paine died in 1809. The author of *The Rights of Man* and *Common Sense* enjoyed a "somewhat Bohemian manner of life," according to one

(Above) Jessie Tarbox Beals. *Greenwich Village Theatre, Sheridan Square.* c. 1919. Photograph. Howard Greenberg Gallery, New York

of his biographers. Thomas Jefferson praised Paine as the only writer in America who could write better than himself.

102 Bedford Street: Twin Peaks was reconstructed in 1925 for artists' housing (ten apartments, each renting for $68.50 a month). There apparently was just one writer and no artists at all among the early tenants.

Grove Court, between Bedford and Hudson Streets: it's said that O. Henry was inspired to write *The Last Leaf* after he'd read Murger's *Scènes de la Vie de Bohème* and been taken to Grove Court to see "the most picturesque bit of rear tenement that remains in New York."

485 Hudson Street: Church of St. Luke's in the Fields, built in 1821. The Parish House was the boyhood home of Bret Harte, author of *The Luck of Roaring Camp.*

86 Bedford Street: Chumley's opened as a speakeasy in 1928 during Prohibition, with a side entrance for fast exits (at 58 Barrow Street). It used to be a literary hangout and the book jackets of the old-time regulars are still on display.

75 1/2 Bedford Street: the poet Edna St. Vincent Millay lived here—and countless other places in the Village, but this is the house with the official plaque.

Beautiful and bohemian, Millay had an intoxicating effect on people. When she first arrived in Greenwich Village at the end of 1917, she performed at the Provincetown Playhouse. "I remember," wrote a playwright, "how in response to a call for the ingenue part, a slender little girl with red-gold hair read the lines . . . and read the lines so winningly that she was at once engaged—at a salary of nothing at all. She left her name and address as she was departing . . . and we wondered if she could possibly be the author of that beautiful and astonishing poem "Renascence."

Her poetry and her own lighthearted boldness made Millay a celebrity. Described by one of her lovers as delightful and charming in matters of the heart but extremely exasperating to any males with possessive instincts, she rued that "My whole life is messed up with people falling in love with me."

One of her conquests was the critic Edmund Wilson, whose journals from the 1920s are laced with *chagrin d'amour* for Millay.

He described the first time he saw her, at a Village party, "dressed in some bright batik, and her face lit up . . . one of those women whose features are not perfect . . . but who, excited by the blood or the spirit, become almost supernaturally beautiful. . . . She had the look of a muse, and her reading of poetry was thrilling."

Edna St. Vincent Millay, the green-eyed gamine who inspired a generation to live fearlessly and fully—at whatever cost—was completely disciplined when writing poems. She herself said that when working she locked herself in her room with several packets of cigarettes and "wrote with the same inspired precision that a sculptor chips marble, spending hours to achieve perfection." ·

(Above) Alexandra Stonehill. Photograph of Grove Court

CROOKED STREETS

"The streets have run crazy and broken themselves into small strips called 'places.' Those places make strange angles and curves. One street crosses itself a time or two."

—*O. Henry*, The Last Leaf

Greenwich Village's maze of winding streets sets it apart from the rest of the city. Rather than adhering to Manhattan's rigid grid pattern, the Village streets follow farm lanes and Indian trails, stagecoach routes and 18th century property lines.

The Commissioners' Plan of 1811 established a matrix of symmetrical streets for the whole city, going from north to south, crossed by parallel streets running from river to river—completely disregarding the natural topography of the island. Residents of nineteenth century Greenwich Village protested vigorously against the grid pattern and succeeded in convincing the city to modify the plan (while also setting a precedent for this community now famous for challenging authority).

The entire Village west of Sixth Avenue was allowed to retain its irregular streetscape.

Today, the old streets with their unconventional patterns have survived as one more example of Village nonconformity.

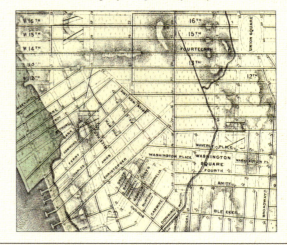

(Above) Egbert L. Viele. *Viele's Water Map*. 1865. Private collection

Millay sent this letter to a poetry editor in 1918:

Spring is here,—and I could be very happy, except that I am broke. Would you mind paying me now instead of on publication for those so stunning verses of mine which you have? I am become very, very thin and have taken to smoking Virginia tobacco.

Wistfully yours,
Edna St. Vincent Millay

P.S. I am awfully broke. Would you mind paying me a lot?

38 Commerce Street: The Cherry Lane Theater is around the corner from the home of Millay, who was one of the founders. Opening in 1924 as a place for experimental plays, the theater staged avant-garde productions such as Samuel Beckett's *Waiting for Godot* and Gertrude Stein's *Doctor Faustus Lights the Lights.*

Greenwich Village was the place to see experimental plays with innovative writing and minimal staging during the early decades of the twentieth century, with Village theaters deliberately presenting an alternative to the conservative and commercial values of the uptown houses. Max Eastman sagely advised the Village producers to "Forget about the box office and adhere to pure standards of art."

50 Commerce Street: the photographer Berenice Abbott's studio was on the fourth floor of this building for nearly thirty years. She moved here in 1935, the same year that she began her series of documentary photographs of New York City.

Abbott had first arrived in Greenwich Village from Ohio in 1918, playing bit parts in Eugene O'Neill's plays and sharing an apartment on MacDougal Street with Djuna Barnes, Malcolm Cowley, and some of the Provincetown Players while she studied to become a sculptor. Marcel Duchamp commissioned her to cast a set of chess pieces and she taught him to dance.

She soon joined the exodus to Paris, with a one-way ticket and $6, and found a job as Man Ray's photo assistant. After three years, she opened her own photography studio and became known as a fashionable portrait photographer.

When she returned to New York in 1929, Abbott was determined to "do in Manhattan what Eugene Atget did in

Paris" and document the city and its state of flux through her photographs. Unable to raise funds for this project, she began teaching the first photography course given by the New School. Her application to photograph the city was eventually accepted by the Federal Art Project of the WPA, with a weekly salary of $145 and an assistant to help carry 60 pounds of equipment about the city. Over 300 of the photographs taken for this project were published in Abbott's comprehensive book *Changing New York*, which was printed just in time for the 1939 World's Fair. Some of the most familiar images show places near the Commerce Street loft where she lived for years with the art critic Elizabeth McCausland: Greenwich Village's Charles Lane, the "El" Station on Christopher Street, Zito's bread store, the Lafayette and Brevoort hotels, Patchin Place. Each photograph portrays change as the central theme, with "the past jostling with the present."

Greenwich Village's bohemian life was recorded by another woman photographer, Jessie Tarbox Beals. A generation older than Abbott, she had arrived in New York in 1905 after crisscrossing the country as a successful newspaper photographer. Beals was inspired by her avant-garde Village neighbors, whom she described as "earnest creative young people making sacrifices to accomplish their dreams." Hauling about an unwieldy 8x10 camera and tripod, she created a Village series depicting artistic people and the places they congregated, from Polly's restaurant to Webster Hall. In 1917, she opened a tearoom and art gallery on Sheridan Square, serving lemonade and strawberry shortcake along with her local scenes.

St. Luke's Place: a small literary colony formed here in 1922, with Sherwood Anderson at No. 12, Marianne Moore two doors away at No. 14 (and working part-time at the Hudson Park public library across the street), and Theodore Dreiser living on the parlor floor at No. 16. St. Luke's Place is still one of the prettiest streets in the Village.

7 Cornelia Street: W. H. Auden resided here for eight years, "sandwiched between sweet-smelling bakeries and salumerias on

this narrow street," before moving to St. Mark's Place. He wrote *Age of Anxiety* here, which could have been purchased at the Phoenix Bookshop—famous for its modern poetry selection—across the way at 18 Cornelia Street during the 1950s and '60s.

A writer described seeing Auden on Cornelia Street, "scurrying along with his arms full of books and papers. He looked like a man running out of a burning building with whatever possessions he'd been able to grab."

161 West 4th Street: Bob Dylan (Robert Allan Zimmerman) was inspired to record one of his greatest hits, "Positively 4th Street" when he lived here during the early 1960s. His career was launched in the nearby Bleecker Street cafes.

18 Gay Street: Mary McCarthy perched here in a tiny studio with a "teetery bookcase" in 1936, while she wrote reviews for *The Nation* and became immersed in the politics of Trotskyism. In the triangular brick building across the street at 165 Waverly Place—originally a medical clinic known as the Northern Dispensary— Edgar Allan Poe was treated for a head cold in 1837.

154 West 10th Street, corner of Waverly Place: Three Lives Bookshop, an oasis of civility. Very literary, appropriately, since it's located on a street named (although persistently misspelled) for Sir Walter Scott's novel *Waverley*.

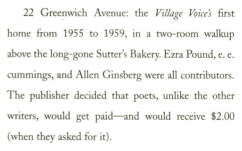

22 Greenwich Avenue: the *Village Voice's* first home from 1955 to 1959, in a two-room walkup above the long-gone Sutter's Bakery. Ezra Pound, e. e. cummings, and Allen Ginsberg were all contributors. The publisher decided that poets, unlike the other writers, would get paid—and would receive $2.00 (when they asked for it).

Intersection of Seventh Avenue and West 12th Street: site of Loew's Sheridan Theater, one of the great movie palaces. In the summer of 1957, the legendary jazz singer Billie Holiday, known as Lady Day, gave a rare New York performance here. Barred from appearing in the city's nightclubs for more than a decade because of drug charges, Holiday could sing here—and

(Above) Alexandra Stonehill. Photograph of Greenwich Village horsewalk

did, after her Philadelphia gig that night. The theater critic of the *Village Voice* had commandeered a powder blue Chrysler for the trip to New York, with Billie holding her chihuahua in one hand and a drink in the other. By the time she walked onto the New York stage, it was nearly 3:00 A.M., but every one of the 2,500 people in the audience (each paying $2.80) had waited to hear her sing.

Corner of 12th Street and Seventh Avenue: St. Vincent's Hospital, the local Village medical center. Jack Kerouac was brought here after a boxer beat him up, Gregory Corso was born here, and—an intrinsic part of literary lore— Dylan Thomas died here after a drunken binge at the nearby White Horse Tavern.

Bank Street: a street that meanders through literary memoirs, just as it actually winds through the West Village, becom-

ing entangled in Abingdon Square and then continuing west to the river. Lionel Trilling and his wife Diana's first apartment was at No.1; later he would remember that "my address was Bank Street, which, of all the famous streets of the Village, seemed to me at the time to have had the most distinguished past."

The writer Allen Tate lived in the basement of 27 Bank Street. Edmund Wilson not only lived on this street but found an apartment there for the narrator in his novel *I Thought of Daisy* (when the young narrator brought home a poet one night, he worried that the apartment was too bourgeois, with its Whistler print and sets of books. "I attempted to call attention to the only feature of the place which might be considered Bohemian and raffish: 'That's not the right time,' I pointed out. 'That clock hasn't gone for years!'")

(Above) Edward Hopper. *The Sheridan Theatre*. 1937. The Newark Museum, Newark, New Jersey

Willa Cather lived at 5 Bank Street from 1913 to 1927, on the second floor of a brownstone furnished with a large etching of George Sand over the fireplace, a marble bust of Keats, and furniture she'd bought at auction rooms on University Place. She wrote three novels here, including the classic *My Antonia.*

Everything in the rooms except the flowers was "simple, plain, all but spartan." In the winter, the apartment was filled with orange blossoms, camellias, violets, freesias. In the spring, jonquils and narcissus stood on the table, and lilac and dogwood branched on the mantel. The front three rooms were used as a large living room for her Friday afternoon teas, when she was at home to visitors (D. H. Lawrence came twice).

The quiet leisurely pace of Bank Street appealed to Cather. In the mornings, she did the marketing, hunting through the nearby Jefferson Market for perfect leaf lettuce, ripe Camembert, and fresh plump chickens that would be prepared for lunch by her French cook Josephine. She wrote for three hours every day, disconnecting her phone when writing. The only sound in

(Above) *Willa Cather.* c. 1904. The Nebraska State Historical Society

the house was overhead, where a German family lived; the daughter diligently practiced the piano, playing Beethoven's *Appassionata* over and over. Cather came to like this, considering it "a signal to work."

Willa Cather was never involved in the vagaries and goings-on of bohemian life in Greenwich Village. This formidable woman, who never had the least little bit of small talk, preferred to concentrate on her work and to live quietly with her companion, Edith Lewis. Cather had wanted to live in her Bank Street apartment for the rest of her life, she told her friends—but she was forced to leave when the building was demolished in 1927.

265 West 11th Street: André Breton, founder of Surrealism, lived here while in exile during World War II (when he returned to France, he was informed that he'd been expelled from the surrealist group. Breton's reply was a shout: "I am surrealism"). Next door, at 263, was where Thomas Wolfe lived in the 1920s. His affection for the house and "its red brick walls, its rooms of noble height and spaciousness, its old dark woods and floors that creaked" was expressed in his novel *You Can't Go Home Again.*

567 Hudson Street: The White Horse Tavern was the destination for many who were making the rounds during the 1950s and 1960s, first to "Julius's for those fat hamburgers on toast, then the San Remo . . . and the White Horse. Booze was a social thing. The bar scene wasn't just to get drunk. It was like the public square in a town or a sidewalk cafe in Paris—comradely meeting and talking." In particular, this was the favorite bar of Dylan Thomas when he was in New York giving his famous poetry readings.

210 West 14th Street: Marcel Duchamp had a studio on the top floor, up four flights of stairs, from 1943 to 1965. Since there was no telephone, visitors wrote to him in advance or called up to him from the street. Robert Motherwell used to have lunch with him at a nearby Italian bistro, where Duchamp always ordered a bowl of plain pasta. Franz Kline's studio was down the street, at 242 West 14th.

THE WATERFRONT

The Hudson River waterfront is where Greenwich Village began. This is the only riverside enclave left in Manhattan that retains much of a nineteenth-century character, with its mixture of residential and commercial properties, and its vistas that connect the land to the sea.

This was where Herman Melville was a customs' inspector on Gansevoort Pier at West Street for nearly twenty years, earning $4.00 a day.

Nearby, at Collier's publishing house at 416 West 13th Street, e. e. cummings worked as a young man, answering letters and sending out book orders.

The Titanic survivors were brought to the Jane Street Hotel at the corner of West and Jane Streets, after disembarking from the White Star Line's Carpathia on Pier 56 at 14th Street, in 1912.

Westbeth, at 463 West Street, was converted to artists' housing in 1970. It is the largest studio building in the world, with a long waiting list of artists who would like to live there.

The poet Robert Lowell was held in the West Side Jail on the corner of 11th and West Street at the beginning of his year's prison sentence in 1943, for refusing to serve in World War II. One of his fellow inmates recalled that Lowell was in a cell next to Lepke of Murder Incorporated, who said to him: "I'm in for killing. What are you in for?" "Oh, I'm in for refusing to kill."

Map Legend: Walk Four

☙ = Structure No Longer Exists

Fourth Avenue Bookstores.
1940s. New York Bound Archives

Walk Four:

ASTOR PLACE and the EAST VILLAGE

This eastern boundary of Greenwich Village is not considered part of the Village by some, yet it too has an extraordinary heritage of artists, writers, and rebels. Imagine Herman Melville, Jack Kerouac, Walt Whitman, and W. H. Auden living in the same neighborhood, blocks from one another, separated only by decades of time.

Visually, it is an area of vivid contrasts: small houses overshadowed by massive loft buildings, historic churches jostling avant-garde clubs. Originally farmland, it rapidly evolved in the nineteenth century from the most fashionable residential area in the city to a busy commercial district of publishing and printing companies. Vestiges of these earlier periods are still visible.

653 Broadway: site of Pfaff's, a lively beer cellar that became the first gathering place in America for bohemians. In the 1850s and early 1860s, writers and actors congregated here to talk all night and consume German wines, beer, beefsteaks, and *pfanne-kuchen*.

This was the rendezvous for many of the contributors of *The Saturday Press*, the bold and controversial magazine that published Walt Whitman's poems and other new American writing. Whitman himself was a regular at Pfaff's, sitting in the alcove at the end of the dim, smoky room where he could "watch and be worshipped." Sometimes he would expand the bohemian circle by inviting Broadway coach drivers and young doctors from New York

MISS CLARE

Hospital to join him here. In his journal he wrote:

> "The vault at Pfaff's
> where the drinkers and laughers
> meet to eat and carouse,
> While on the walk immediately overhead
> pass the myriad feet of Broadway."

The most dramatic member of the Pfaffian circle was unquestionably Ada Clare, the flamboyant actress, writer, and feminist known as the Queen of Bohemia. Although she had published her first poem to great acclaim when she was only nineteen, she later had less success at novel writing and acting.

Few women ventured into Pfaff's, but Ada Clare held court there, spending the evenings smoking and drinking and talking brilliantly. She had numerous lovers and might have been describing herself when she wrote that "the Bohemian is not, like the creature of society, a victim of rules and customs."

Ada Clare died horribly, after being bitten by a rabid dog at her theatrical agent's office. Walt Whitman, who knew her well at Pfaff's, wrote to a friend: "Poor, poor Ada Clare—I have been inexpressibly shocked by the horrible and sudden close of her gay, easy, sunny, free, loose, but not ungood life."

29 East 4th Street: the 1832 Merchant's House Museum is a stopping-off place into a past century, when this was an exclusive neighborhood. The Tredwell family lived here for nearly one hundred years—and some of their books are still in the bookcase, waiting to be read again. There are five volumes of Washington Irving's *Life of George Washington*, some nineteenth-century romantic novels and French phrase books, Addison and Steele's *Essays* from the *Spectator*, and an etiquette book, *The Habits of Good Society*.

425 Lafayette Street: The Astor Library was the first free public library in the city, although the public was not encouraged to browse. When it opened in 1854, the library housed the largest collection of books in America—100,000 volumes, all uncatalogued. Now the acclaimed Public Theater, pro-ductions were first presented here in 1966 by the legendary theater producer Joseph Papp. One of its early productions was *Hair,* performed in what had been the library's main reading room.

Across the street at 428–434 Lafayette is Colonnade Row, also known as LaGrange Terrace, which was originally a row of nine elegant houses (only four remain). Washington Irving lived here when the houses were first built in 1833.

Astor Place was the scene of a ferocious riot in 1849, provoked by a long-standing feud between two Shakespearean actors. Supporters of the American actor Edwin Forrest interrupted the performance of his English rival William Macready at the Astor Place Opera House, where he was playing the title role in *Macbeth*. Thousands of rioters milled outside the theater, heaving paving stones at the mounted police and leaving the opera house in shambles. It was the second-most serious riot in the city's history, with twenty-two killed and hundreds wounded.

(Above) The Merchant's House Museum vintage postcard

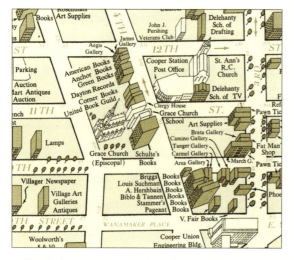

Fourth Avenue: the stretch from Astor Place to 14th Street was known for many years as "Booksellers Row." With nearly two dozen second-hand booksellers located here in the 1940s, this was New York's version of the bookstalls along the Seine's *quais*.

Fashionable bookstores were located near the many prestigious libraries in Astor Place during the 1850s and secondhand dealers eventually moved nearby. Jacob Abrahams was the first to establish a secondhand bookstore in this area, in 1893; within a decade, there were seven others. By the time the telephone company issued its first Yellow Pages in 1928, there were nineteen booksellers listed with a Fourth Avenue address.

A number of the bookstores banded together in 1942 to issue a cooperative catalogue of a thousand titles from their very diverse stocks of out-of-print and rare books. By the 1950s and '60s, however, Fourth Avenue had become such valuable real estate that these low-rent bookshops—their sidewalk tables piled high with inexpensive books—were forced to close down or move.

The only bookshop now on this street is the tiny Alabaster at 122 Fourth Avenue. Just around the corner is the gargantuan Strand, at 828 Broadway at 12th Street, which stocks more than eight miles of used and new books.

103 Fourth Avenue: Newly married, Herman Melville and his wife Lizzie lived at this location (the building has since been demolished) from 1847 to 1849, within walking distance of the

(Above) Map of Fourth Avenue. 1961. New York Bound Archives

theaters on Astor Place. Mrs. Melville, a Bostonian, worried that life in New York was too pleasurable: "Tonight we go to the Opera. We have resolved to stop after this though and not go out at all . . . if Herman does not get a full night's rest or indulges in a late supper, he does not feel right for writing the next day."

A voracious reader, Melville often walked over to East 8th Street (then called Clinton Place) to borrow books from Evert Duyckinck, a literary patron who was known for his library of 18,000 volumes as well as for introducing writers to each other at his Saturday night suppers (Melville met Washington Irving here).

Melville was completing *Redburn* and *White Jacket* while he lived on Fourth Avenue, working in his third-floor study. His sea-tale *Mardi* was published during this time, with sales of 2,154 books the first year—but Melville had overdrawn his account at his publisher and was left with a debt of $733.

108 Fourth Avenue: the classic Beat film *Pull My Daisy*—written by Jack Kerouac—was shot in a loft here in late 1958. The cast consisted of some of the *real* Beat writers and their friends (Gregory Corso portrayed Jack Kerouac, Larry Rivers played Neal Cassady, and Allen Ginsberg was himself).

This black-and-white twenty-eight minute film was completed in two weeks, on a $15,000 budget. The film's narrative was recorded afterwards by Kerouac. None of the participants expected this to become "the classic, underground, out-of-focus beatnik epic."

The year before, in 1957, Kerouac had published *On the Road*, the picaresque novel that made him—and the Beat Generation—forever famous. This young unknown author became an overnight sensation after the *New York Times* book review raved that "Just as *The Sun Also Rises* came to be regarded as the testament of the 'Lost Generation,' so it seems certain that *On the Road* will come to be known as that of the 'Beat Generation.'"

(Above) *Herman Melville.* **Private collection**

Part of Kerouac's success was that he appeared to be a romantic bohemian (one of his girlfriends said that he looked like a movie star, with a combination of irresistible innocence and wildness). His earliest literary influence was Thomas Wolfe and, in the same way as Wolfe, he thought of all his novels as a single autobiographical story. Critics pointed out that Kerouac's spontaneous writing had a counterpart in the improvisational jazz and the abstract expressionist paintings being created in Greenwich Village during this time.

The Village was a hangout for Kerouac, rather than a place to live. He drank at the White Horse, listened to jazz at the Five Spot, visited friends on Grove or Bedford Street, read his work at the Village Vanguard, and described the hipster scenes at the San Remo in his book *The Subterraneans.*

In the Sixties, anyone who wanted to be hip, or cool, or simply rebellious, used Kerouac's *On the Road* as a guidebook. And the East Village was their main destination: they hitchhiked here in jeans, black turtlenecks, berets, and sandals, smoking marijuana, listening to jazz, and talking about existentialism. One of the original Beats would later say that "Kerouac opened a million coffee bars and sold a million pair of Levis."

119 East 11th Street: Webster Hall was the scene of all-night masquerade balls from 1913 through the early 1930s, inextricably adding to Greenwich Village's reputation as a bohemian place of merrymaking.

Ironically, the first ball held at Webster Hall—in 1913—was organized for a serious cause. In order to raise money for the radical publication *The Masses* (which was continually in desperate financial straits even though none of the contributors were ever paid), the editors decided to organize a fancy dress party that would be patterned after the Parisian *bal masqués*. Searching for a suitable dance hall, they talked to the owner of Webster Hall, who also owned the bar next door. "Is yours a drinking crowd?" he asked the editors. "Hell, yes," was the truthful reply. In that case, they were told, they could have the hall without charge.

The Masses ball was so successful that it became the beginning of what seemed an endless number of all-night parties with various themes: Pagan Romps, Art Model Frolics, and homosexual revels were so popular that by 1918 there were as many as two balls a week. Admission in the early years was $1 for those in costume and $2 for those without, which guaranteed that the Villagers would arrive as sheiks, smock-clad artists, circus dancers, cavemen, and skimpy-skirted ballerinas. The disguises created an anonymity that allowed the carousers to be even bolder and more flamboyant in their escapades at Webster Hall.

"So the Greenwich Villager sets out to amuse himself. It's sordid and hard, but it must be done," wrote Djuna Barnes, sardon-

(Above) John Sloan. *Costume Ball Poster*. 1933. The Whitney Museum of American Art

ically describing a Greenwich Village ball. "By two and two they come, pompous beetles in the web of an old desire. They pass up the stairs, are seen walking through the gallery arm in arm, painted faces and painted skins, painted limbs and painted fans, telling each other the things in life that mean little and much."

Broadway and 10th Street: The most fashionable church in New York in the nineteenth century was Grace Church, the splendid 1846 Gothic Revival structure designed by James Renwick. A society publication of the time reported that New York's proper people "keep carriages, live above Bleecker Street, are subscribers to the opera, go to Grace Church, have a town house and a country house."

Across the street from Grace Church, at 785 Broadway, was the site of Matthew Brady's photo studio from 1860 until 1871 when he was forced into bankruptcy from debts he'd incurred documenting the Civil War.

A century later, during the early 1960s, the poet and art curator Frank O'Hara lived nearby in a floor-through loft at 791 Broadway. "He'd finish poems and put them anyplace," a friend

(Above) Grace Church vintage postcard

remembered. "His typewriter was always on his kitchen table . . . as pieces got done they just wandered anywhere. The towel drawer was a very good place." Writing directly from his life and experience, O'Hara—part of the New York School of Poetry—created what he called "personal poems."

10th Street between Third and Fourth Avenue: during the mid-1950s, when this area was beginning to be known as the East Village, many of the younger artists had their studios here. Willem de Kooning lived at 88 East 10th Street and more than a dozen other artists lived on the same block. Cooperative galleries—the Tanager, Camino, Area, March, and Brata, among others—were organized by the artists, often with joint Friday night gallery openings that included poetry readings and jazz.

118 East 10th Street: the childhood home of legendary architect Stanford White, who created Beaux Arts grandeur in turn-of-the-century New York. The critic Lewis Mumford paid tribute to White's designs in Greenwich Village: "the campanile of the Judson Memorial Church rising like a gracious rebuke to the uncivilized modern chapel next to it; the buoyant limestone spring of the Washington Arch launching Fifth Avenue on its northward course; the Church of the Ascension's chancel wall of quarried honey."

Corner of 10th Street and Second Avenue: St. Mark's-in-the-Bowery Church—built in 1799, with a steeple and portico added later—has long been associated with creative spirits: Isadora Duncan danced here, William Carlos Williams read his poetry, Frank Lloyd Wright lectured about architecture (and proposed designs for three apartment buildings that would have towered over the church). The renowned St. Mark's Poetry Project began organizing readings in the mid-1960s.

Second Avenue became known as the Jewish Rialto during the 1920s, when the street was burgeoning with nearly twenty Yiddish-language theaters (and restaurants serving Russian, Polish, Hungarian, and Romanian specialties). The Café Royale—once located on the southeast corner of East 12th Street—was known as the artistic and intellectual center of the Yiddish-speaking world in America. A local journalist described it as "an enclave where artists, actors, and writers came to debate, over endless glasses of tea, the great questions of art that have gone unanswered in every civilized language."

Across the street, The Yiddish Art Theater at 189 Second Avenue, eventually metamorphosed into the Phoenix Theater in the 1950s, producing avant-garde plays and revivals (Montgomery Cliff starred in Chekhov's *The Sea Gull* in 1954) and still later became a movie theater.

208 East 13th Street: Emma Goldman lived here from 1903 to 1912, publishing the anarchist journal *Mother Earth*. Whether she was lecturing at Carnegie Hall or in Mabel Dodge's living room, the fearless and outspoken Goldman crusaded for equal rights for women, free love, tolerance of homosexuality, trade unionism, and other radical causes. Arrested for advocating birth control, she was given a banquet at the Brevoort organized by John Sloan (although he admitted that her earnestness wore him down). She was deported to Russia in 1919 along with a number of other radicals.

St. Mark's Place is full of interesting juxtapositions. In 1834, James Fenimore Cooper spent a quiet winter at No. 6 (and the

The National Theatre Management and All Star Cast Arriving at their New Permanent Home, Kessler Second Avenue Theatre, Second Avenue and Second Street.

A. Lebedeff, L. Blank, L. Levin, P. Graff, B. Rosenthal, V. Luboff, A. Thomashefsky, M. Rosenblatt, S. Gertler, P. Klids, S. Schorr, N. Dranova, A. Hoffman, M. Wilensky, I. Lash, I. Trilling and our Warsaw Comedian, Itzchok Feld, M. Saks, General Manager; Ph. Schneider, Business Manager, H. Wohl, Composer.   RAPPAPORT STUDIO

(Above) Second Avenue Theatre cast. 1920. Yivo Institute

summer in Queens, sailing to Astoria on a sloop). In the next century, during the 1960s, this was the wildest street in the Village: at No. 4, improvised multimedia events described as 'Happenings' were being created by Claes Oldenburg, Robert Rauschenberg, and Jim Dine, while across the street, at No. 23, the nightclub Dom was rented by Andy Warhol for hip performances. This was the center of an uninhibited counterculture, thriving on "marijuana, jazz, not much money, and a community of feeling that society is the prison of the nervous system."

This was also the street where the poet W. H. Auden lived from 1953 to 1972, at 77 St. Mark's Place, during each fall and winter. The previous tenant of his old-fashioned railroad apartment had been an abortionist—and occasionally jittery people knocked on the door, asking for the doctor. It was also the same building where Leon Trotsky had printed *Novy Mir* when he lived in New York.

Auden's writing table was piled with papers and manuscripts in wild disarray, nearly covering his pale blue Olympia portable

(Right) *W. H. Auden*. 1969. Corbis

typewriter. He worked in the front parlor, a high-ceilinged room with a green-marbled fireplace and a small watercolor by Blake hanging slightly askew above the bookcases.

He insisted on keeping his telephone number in the Manhattan directory and would agree to see almost anyone who called him up. Just outside his door, St. Mark's Place was a mecca for the beatnik invasion—but Auden lived with aplomb in the middle of this frenzy.

Cooper Square: best described as not "a square but a long triangle, its base the old brown Cooper Union building, like a hand-tinted rotogravure on the blue winter sky." The

main building of Cooper Union—the renowned college of art, architecture, and engineering—contains the Great Hall where many writers and politicians have given speeches. Mark Twain gave his first New York lecture here in May 1867 (tickets were fifty cents and few were sold, so the house was papered by giving tickets to schoolteachers). The most famous oration ever given here was Abraham Lincoln's "Right Makes Might" speech, which is credited with winning him the presidential nomination.

The little park on Cooper Square has a sculpture by Augustus Saint-Gaudens showing Peter Cooper seated (although Cooper spent so many afternoons in McSorley's back room that he was given a chair of his own over there).

15 East 7th Street, just off Cooper Square: McSorley's Old Ale House opened in 1854 and for years has claimed to be the oldest saloon in the city. Even during Prohibition, McSorley's never closed nor was it ever raided, although the ale had to be surreptitiously produced in a row of washtubs in the cellar. Its motto was "Good ale, raw onions, and no ladies" until 1971, when women finally gained admittance. John Sloan painted five canvases of the saloon between 1912 and 1930, showing the dark interior frozen in time.

(Opposite) John Sloan. *McSorley's Bar.* **1912. The Detroit Institute of Arts**
(Above) Etching of Cooper Union. Private collection

LIST OF
ILLUSTRATIONS

·ᘒᘖᘗᘙ·

Page 52. Alexandra Stonehill. Photograph of Tenth Street townhouse

Page 53. Berenice Abbott. *Greenwich Village, Thirty-Four Studios, 51 West 10th Street*. 1938. The Museum of the City of New York. Commerce Graphics Ltd, Inc.

Page 54. Al Hirschfeld. *Joe Gould*. c. 1942. Lithograph. Art reproduced by special arrangement with Al Hirschfeld's exclusive representative, The Margo Feiden Galleries Ltd., New York

Page 55. Alexandra Stonehill. A nineteenth-century book from the Salmagundi Club library. Photographed by permission of the Salmagundi Club

Page 57. Jessie Tarbox Beals. *The Lair of Clivette in Sheridan Square*. c. 1910–17. Photograph. Howard Greenberg Gallery, New York

Page 58. John Sloan. *Jefferson Market*. 1917, retouched 1922. Oil on canvas. The Pennsylvania Academy of the Fine Arts. Henry D. Gilpin Fund

Page 59. Jefferson Market. 1904. New York Bound Archives

Page 60. John Sloan painting on the canvas of *Buses in the Square*. c. 1927. Helen Farr Sloan Library. Delaware Art Museum

Page 61. Alexandra Stonehill. Artist's palette from the Salmagundi Club collection. Photographed by permission of the Salmagundi Club

Page 62. e. e. cummings. *Self-portrait*. c. 1940. Corbis

Page 64. Edward Hopper. *Early Sunday Morning*. 1930. Oil on canvas. Whitney Museum of American Art. Purchase, with funds from Gertrude Vanderbilt Whitney

Page 65. Jessie Tarbox Beals. *Greenwich Village Theatre, Sheridan Square*. c. 1919. Photograph. Howard Greenberg Gallery, New York

Page 66. Arnold Genthe. *Edna St. Vincent Millay*. 1913 or 1914. Photograph. The New-York Historical Society

Page 67. Alexandra Stonehill. Photograph of Grove Court

Page 68. Egbert L. Viele. Viele's Water Map. 1865. Private collection

Page 71. John Sloan. *Carmine Theater*. 1912. Hirshhorn Museum and Sculpture Garden, Smithsonian Institution. Gift of the Joseph H. Hirshhorn Foundation, 1966. Photographer, Lee Stalsworth

Page 72. Alexandra Stonehill. Photograph of Greenwich Village horsewalk

Page 73. Edward Hopper. *The Sheridan Theatre*. 1937. Oil on canvas. The Newark Museum, New Jersey. Copyright The Newark Museum/Art Resource, New York

Page 74. *Willa Cather*. c. 1904. The Nebraska State Historical Society

Page 76. Alexandra Stonehill. Photographs of cobblestone pavement in Gansevoort Market and Jane Street Hotel

Page 77. Lee Krasner. *Gansevoort*. 1934. The Metropolitan Museum of Art. Gift of the Pollock-Krasner Foundation, Inc., 1997. (1997.403.1) Photograph © 1998 The Metropolitan Museum of Art. Copyright The Pollock-Krasner Foundation/Artists Rights Society (ARS), New York

Page 79. Fourth Avenue Bookstores. 1940s. New York Bound Archives

Page 80. Rudy Burckhardt. *Astor Place*. c. 1948. Gelatin Silver Print. Tibor de Nagy Gallery, New York

Page 81. Franz Kline. *Wanamaker Block*. 1955. Yale University Art Gallery. Gift of Richard Brown Baker, B.A. 1935

Page 82. *Ada Clare*. Harvard Theatre Collection. The Houghton Library. Harvard University

Page 83. The Merchant's House Museum vintage postcard. Private collection

Page 84. Map of Fourth Avenue. 1961. New York Bound Archives

Page 85. *Herman Melville*. Private collection

Page 86. Allen Ginsberg. *Jack Kerouac at 206 East 7th Street*. 1953. Photograph. The Allen Ginsberg Trust

Page 87. John Sloan. *Costume Ball Poster*. 1933. The Whitney Museum of American Art

Page 88. Grace Church vintage postcard. Private collection

Page 89. Revelers at Webster Hall. Private collection

Page 90. Second Avenue Theatre cast. 1920. Yivo Institute

Page 91. *W. H. Auden*. 1969. Corbis.

Page 92. John Sloan. *McSorley's Bar*. 1912. The Detroit Institute of Arts. Founders Society Purchase, General Membership Fund

Page 93. Etching of Cooper Union: Founders' Hall. Private collection.

Page 96. Saul Steinberg. *8th Street*. 1966. Collage of watercolor and ink on paper. Grey Art Gallery, New York University Art Collection. Anonymous gift, 1968

Front cover: Vintage postcard of Washington Square. Private collection

Back cover: Panoramic View of Washington Square. c. 1910. New York Bound Archives

Title page: Washington Square. c. 1900. New York Bound Archives

Endpapers: "The Row," Washington Square North. 1981. Photo by Andrew Rasiej